Regulation: Audit, Inspection, Standards and Risk

A Handbook

For

Street-Level Regulators

John Brady

Amy Brady

Precepts Books

Precepts Books

First published by Precepts Books, Ireland 2014

Second Edition June 2016

Email: **info@precepts.eu**

Website: **www.precepts.eu**

The authors hereby assert their moral right to be identified as the creators of 'Regulation: Audit, Inspection, Standards and Risk', as may be required by any laws in any countries in the world.

Credits

Editing Services Ireland

ISBN: 9780993082238

Illustrations

Cover: Water Fountain, Lismore, Ireland. Copyright John Brady

Back Cover: Child Labour, CCO 1.0 Universal (CCO 1.0)

Derived from: https://pixabay.com/en/child-labor-historic-people-349970/

■ CONTENTS

■ LIST OF FIGURES

■ LIST OF TABLES

Introduction

We have all, at some time or another, made contact with street-level regulators. They visit regulated organisations, make decisions on compliance, assess ability, willingness and intention and persuade change. The phrase 'street-level regulator' has its origins in the work of Lipsky (2010), who drew attention to the way in which social and economic policies, however well implemented, rely on particular people to deliver them at the messy level of the street.

In this book, we explore how the street-level regulator copes with the commonplace dilemmas of the job:

- Making consistent judgements
- Working with people to improve outcomes
- Keeping up with essential knowledge
- Recognising the public interest
- Collecting reliable evidence
- Managing relationships fairly
- Gauging the limits of trust.

In short, we explore the everyday practice of being a street-level regulator:

> the day-to-day of practice focuses our attention on the technical, the skills, the attributes and, perhaps most important, the ethics at play in the world of the street-level (regulator). Instead of the abstract and distant world of policy- making ... it places the real world of the street at its heart. And, as such, it shifts our focus from the context-free discussion of theory and ideas ... towards the core professional disciplines and skills. But it also takes us further, to the context-dependent ethics of public service ... It challenges us all to think about what we understand to be knowledge in our discipline. It not only legitimises experience as a source of learning, it places that experience at the centre and asks us to think about our responsibilities (Rowe, 2012: p. 15).

Our Focus

We focus on the core generic skills and knowledge required by those on the regulatory front line. They may audit or inspect businesses, factories, hospitals or wherever there is regulation. They may be called inspectors, surveyors, supervisors, accreditors, auditors, compliance officers, reviewers, assessors, evaluators or scrutineers. We define them all as street-level regulators.

Contents of the Book

At the heart of the book is a step-by-step account of an audit or inspection. The first chapter introduces a model of audit and inspection – Plan, Inspect and Improve. The next two chapters deal with standards and risk. The final three chapters consider the practice of planning, inspecting and improvement.

Chapter 1: The 'Plan, Inspect, Improve' PII inspection model

Regulation does nothing if it does not fix the problems it is supposed to fix. This model emphasises that the results – or outcomes – of regulation and audit are the bottom line. Regulation should add value through improvement.

Chapter 2: Regulation and Standards

The chapter begins by defining regulation in the context of global private standards, risk-assessment and self-regulation. Regulation is no longer the preserve of state or government agencies. Self-regulation has brought with it responsibility by firms for quality management, regulation and safety systems. Accreditation and government regulators are the means of accountability.

Standards give the essential criteria in making decisions on the performance and compliance of organisations. 'Systems theory' is a way to understand types of standards, including flexible standards, and their relationship to outcomes. Finally, the strengths and weaknesses of these different types of standards are examined together with a review of grading/star ratings.

Chapter 3: Risk-based Regulation

Risk is defined using the notions of harm and opportunity and both approaches are central to enterprise. Included are ways to calculate high, medium and low risk, a typical Enterprise Risk-management model and its relevance to regulation and audit. Finally, risk-management tools are reviewed.

Chapter 4: Plan

The key to successful inspection and audit is in the planning. This chapter begins with a risk-assessment of the organisation and identifies the main issues using Pyramid Planning. Evidence criteria and information-collection are set out and examples given of inspection and audit plans. 'Working with people' is a theme and there are sections on whistleblowing and identifying the beneficiaries of the inspection/audit. Finally, common risks are anticipated, such as regulatory capture and ritualistic compliance.

Chapter 5: Inspect

The chapter stresses the importance of the first meeting. It then moves on to the different information-collection methods, such as interview, documents, observation and their strengths and weaknesses, including taking a critical attitude to sources. The methodical collection of evidence is promoted through checking for accuracy, bias and interpretation - in the process, triangulation, drilling-down and case tracking are explained. A section on contemporaneous note-taking further supports the effective collection of evidence and a section on analysis gives a wider understanding of the performance of the organisation.

Chapter 6: Improve

The chapter begins with an examination of what is meant by improvement. A further section addresses the judgement of compliance and the criteria used. The inspection/audit plan supports the structure of this stage in addressing issues and risks in the final conference feedback; again, the importance of relationships is stressed. Responsive and Smart Regulation are explained, the importance of procedural justice approaches reinforced and models of enforcement compared. The final sections include report writing, action planning and methodical follow-up.

Education and Training for Regulators

Figure 1: Specialist Skills and Generic Skills

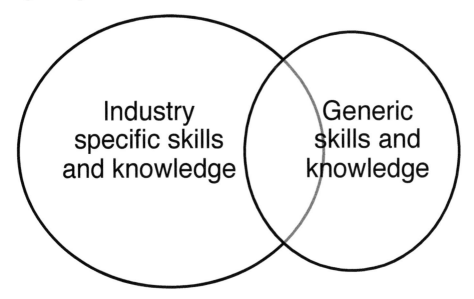

Implementing regulation requires specialist sector knowledge, supported by generic skills and competencies. We are not saying that the only skills needed are generic. Quite the contrary, regulatory judgements are complex and a high level of professional and occupational knowledge is required *as well as* generic skills and knowledge.

Appendix One: The appendix has details of curricula and competence schemes targeted at street-level regulators.

Chapter One: The (PII) Model

Figure 2: The Plan, Inspect, Improve Model (PII)

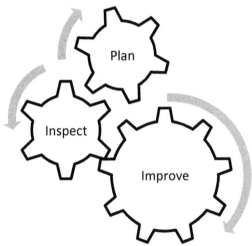

This book is structured on a model of inspection/audit we call *Plan, Inspect, Improve* or PII. It is designed to achieve compliance and improvement, not to meet inspection/audit targets or to hand out violation notices:

> I direct you to change the way you measure the performance of both your agency and your frontline regulators so as to focus on results, not process and punishment. ... You should identify appropriate performance measures and prepare a draft in clear, understandable terms, of the results you are seeking to achieve through your regulatory program (Clinton, 1995).

As President Clinton recognised, evaluating the impact of regulation should be in terms of outcomes and not the number of inspections or audits completed, licences withdrawn or the number of enforcement notices issued. The latter are measures of the regulators 'process and punishment' and not the actual *outcomes* of regulation:

Evaluating the outcomes of regulation is complex, however:

> at its most basic level, inspection seeks to change behaviour in order to produce desired outcomes. When inspection stems from a good faith effort to advance the public interest, those desired outcomes will be improvements in problematic conditions in the world. Inspection — 'works' when it solves, or at least reduces or ameliorates, the problem or problems that prompted government to adopt it in the first place (Coglianese, 2012: p. 9).

Ensuring that regulation 'works' in this way relies on the regulator keeping in mind the initial problem that the legislation or standards aim to deal with. To achieve this, we adapt the Deming framework of continuous improvement (Plan, Do, Check, Act) (Deming, 1986) to a three-stage model Plan, Inspect and Improve. Consequently, improvement becomes the objective.

Explaining the PII Stages

The Plan Stage is more than simply an aide-memoire of what the regulator will do. Analysis using Pyramid Planning reveals the links between your main investigative questions and the relevant criteria. These criteria link, in turn, those questions to the necessary evidence and to the means of information-collection. There is a clear linking of the questions asked to the evidence collected. This analysis (the Plan) guides the next two stages of Inspect and Improve.

Planning is also about being prepared for common regulatory problems such as ritual compliance and regulatory capture as well as the more mundane but vital tasks of communication and coordination of the event.

The Inspect Stage might also have been called the **Audit Stage** or the **Investigation Stage**. Here, the main task is Information Collection. The information you seek dictates the collection method used. Topics include the following:

- Interviews
- Observation
- Questionnaires
- Testing
- Note-taking, including contemporaneous notes and witness statements.

A number of tools support information-collection, such as triangulation, which improves data accuracy. The PII model includes methods that both avoid bias and recognise the significance of the evidence collected.

The Improve Stage focuses on the relationships between regulator and company or organisation, which enables constructive discussion of the Inspect Stage findings. Key factors of compliance will guide your final decisions together with the consideration of hard and soft enforcement and the use of other forms of regulation as levers. The Improve stage concludes with report-writing and an expanded section on follow-up.

Not a Straitjacket

As with any ideal-type model, it provides a direction, not a blueprint – it must be used flexibly, keeping in mind that the point is Improvement. The results of one inspection or audit feed into the next and each becomes part of a cycle of improvement.

These are ideal stages and you can deviate from them.

Aiming for Improvement

The model aims for improvement either through fixing problems or by contributing to the organisation's improvement strategies. That regulation might improve an organisation may puzzle you as the majority of literature conventionally presents regulation as a burden or inconvenience (see Malloy, 2010 for a critique). However, emerging research suggests that this conventional view is exaggerated (Carter et al., 2009). It is argued that inspection, audit and regulation actually *enable* markets:

> Without a comprehensive framework of regulation, market relations of the scale and complexity evident in developed economies today would be impossible (Kitching et al., 2013: p. 7).

Improvement, however, is not just about enabling markets. It also contributes to reducing risks, protecting people and promoting environmental, ethical and conservation principles.

Essential Knowledge

This book takes you through an inspection/audit, from initial planning through to the final report. The first two chapters contain essential background knowledge and it is to this we now turn.

Chapter Two: Regulation and Standards

Objectives

After reading this chapter, you will be able to:

- Define regulation
- Understand the significance of changes in regulation
- Reference your work to a legal or other framework
- Recognise different types of standards and their strengths and weaknesses
- Use standards to set expectations of those you regulate
- Clarify your regulatory powers and when to use them
- Analyse your sector using Systems Theory
- Develop the skills necessary for standards implementation.

Rationale

We define regulation in the context of street-level work. Three different types of regulatory bodies are identified – government, private and civil. These bodies use their own sets of standards that work together in a web of regulation. The notion of public interest is examined together with commentary on the limits of centralised state regulation. The chapter looks at the different types of standards, exploring their strengths and weaknesses. It also introduces you to Systems Theory, an important analytic tool in understanding and implementing standards. The chapter's final section discusses grading.

What is Regulation?

There are many definitions of regulation (see Baldwin et al., 2012: p. 3). For the purposes of this book, regulation is the use of:

> rules, as well as the monitoring and enforcement of these rules by social, business, and political actors on other social, business, and political actors (Levi-Faur, 2011: p. 4).

This definition of regulation may be different from the one you are familiar with - it views regulation, not as an activity solely performed by state agencies, but shared with private agencies that make rules. For example, international standards bodies such as the International Organization for Standardization (ISO) provide standards for business *and* public organisations (ISO Central Secretariat, 2008). Firms use international standards because they want to sell in foreign markets:

> How do standards impact our ability to compete internationally? . . . When we have domestic standards that are different from international standards, everybody loses. We lose domestically because we must build a product that is different from products we sell internationally. That raises . . . [our production] costs, hurt[ing] American consumers . . . [and] caus[ing for us] unfavourable opportunities in foreign markets (Büthe and Mattli, 2011: p. 5).

There are also civil regulators that apply ethical rules to global manufacture and trade. FairTrade and the ethical certification for wood products (Vogel, 2006) are good examples.

All three regulatory bodies above have independent authority and different powers of enforcement and persuasion. However, there is overlap. State regulatory bodies may accept private standards as compliant with their own regulations (Büthe and Mattli, 2011: p. 1). Private companies also conform to civil standards such as factory working conditions because they do not want their reputation damaged (Weil, 2005).

Figure 3: Overlapping Regulatory Bodies

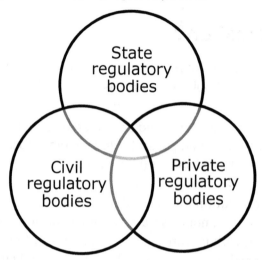

Even in 2003 over 80% of global trade, worth $4 trillion, used international standards (Mattli and Büthe). The pharmaceutical industry, for example, consists of multinational companies selling products in almost every country. There is no one national regulatory framework that will satisfy every country where their products are sold. Consequently, international standards enable these manufacturers to sell their products worldwide.

Market-Driven

The internationalization of private standards is mirrored across multiple industries. The change is market-driven (Mennicken, 2010) – consumers and producers prefer to trade in products that have proven quality, safety and ethical production. Businesses are demonstrating these parameters through regulation – products and systems are audited internally and accredited externally by international standard agencies and state regulatory bodies. Figure 4 shows how the three types of regulatory body interact in regulating a large international pharmaceutical company.

The Web of Regulation

A pharmaceutical company may be regulated by the United States Food and Drugs Administration (USFDA), use guidelines and standards prepared by the International Conference on Harmonisation of Technical Requirements for Registration of Pharmaceuticals for Human Use (ICH) and adopt recommendations from a civil group such as Health Action International. A further level of regulation is a company's own internal audit system, which ensures compliance with the standards and regulations.

Figure 4: Showing Three Types of Regulatory Body and Internal Audit

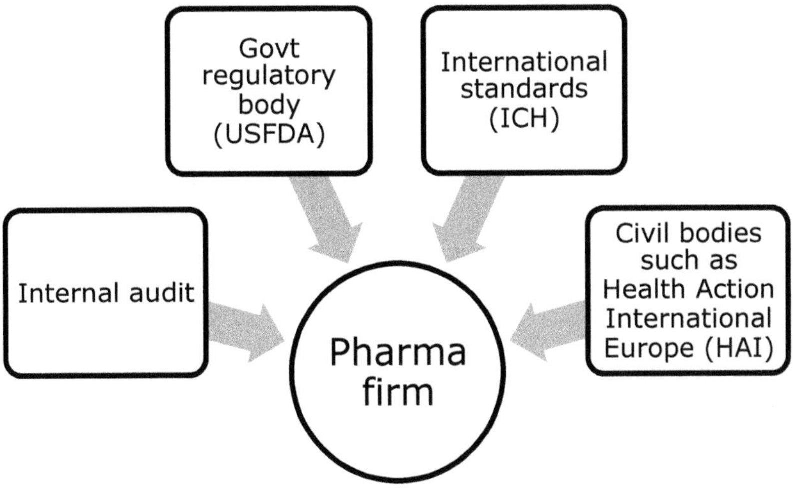

Regulation involves civil, state and business actors at national, local and global levels (Bartley, 2011). It is an overlapping and interlocking web of regulation made effective by the power of reputation in the civil and private sphere and by state enforcement.

> Apply to your work
>
> List the types of regulatory bodies in your sector i.e. civil, governmental and private. What standards are used in your sector and do they overlap?

Regulation is About Improving Outcomes

Regulation, in our definition, aims to change behaviour to achieve better outcomes (Koop and Lodge, 2015). Regulatory bodies intervene directly by employing standards, by monitoring and by persuading compliance with methods such as withdrawing licences, naming-and-shaming and disclosing information through grading and reports. In the case of civil regulatory bodies, some use standards and monitoring, disclosure and either/or political and civil influence.

Not every regulated sector will have to deal directly with international standards and civil regulation. However, even those that might appear confined to a domestic market, such as assisted conception clinics, will have to respond to guidelines from civil bodies. They will also have to adhere to international standards governing their activities and sources of supply such as sources of human tissue (European Parliament and the Council, 2004).

The Public Interest

Regulation exists in most cases because it is in the public interest to oversee certain products, services and relationships. Although there is debate on what 'public interest' means (Feintuck, 2005), most people define it as being for the good of all rather than a minority.

We expect regulation to:

- Provide protection for citizens, for example, food safety, safeguarding older people from abuse
- Assure consumers of fair dealing, e.g. making sure that goods and services are as described
- Act as a deterrent to those who might provide shoddy goods and abusive or dangerous services by incurring punishments such as fines, sanctions, imprisonment and removal of trading-essential accreditation (Boyne et al., 2002)
- Acknowledge and provide publicity for those who provide excellent goods and services.

There are also expectations that regulatory bodies will:

- Raise quality by guidance on better processes for providing goods and services, e.g. complying with a specified quality management system
- Implement standards and monitoring to ensure ethical conduct as in fair labour practices (Toffel et al., 2015) and certification schemes e.g. organic production (Bartley and Smith, 2010).

> Apply to your work
>
> How does your regulatory body further the public interest?

Regulatory Control and Self-Regulation

At the same time, it is accepted that total control through government regulation has difficulties:

- Rules are either too rigid or too flexible
- Most businesses and organisations are better able than regulators to adapt to new technologies and innovative corporate models
- Regulators do not have the resources (time and money) to be everywhere all the time (Sinclair, 1997).

To overcome these difficulties, regulatory bodies encourage firms and organisations to manage their own regulation and then audit to see that the firm's specific compliance systems are working. Where they are not and where the spirit of the law is not being followed, enforcement is then deemed necessary (Gunningham, 2010). This trend applies equally to sectors that perform public services such as the provision and maintenance of care homes and hospitals; the expectation is that organisations will have effective management systems and competent personnel.

The Elements of Regulation

Regulation and accreditation may use:

- *Guidance* to enable organisations to know what is required of them
- Processes that *licence or register* organisations
- Regulations and standards enabling the *measurement* of the degree to which requirements are achieved
- In some cases, *powers* available to the regulator to do their job
- *Sanctions, fines and punishments* that a regulator or auditor might use to persuade, deter or enforce an organisation to meet the requirements
- *Written and public reports* to name, shame and praise organisations for their performance
- *Gradings* to place regulated organisations in a rank order available to the public.

In this chapter, we focus on guidance, legislation, regulations, standards and grading.

Guidance

Nearly all regulatory bodies - government, private or civil - provide early guidance to organisations in plain language. The pressure for plain language in regulation has grown consistently across Europe, Australia and the US (for example, Mandelkern, 2001). Organisations inspected or audited must have easily-accessible and understandable information on expected requirements. The standards used, as well as any associated legislation, is normally available through regulatory websites, or face-to-face, telephone or email queries.

Businesses have encouraged the availability of guidance as inspection or audit represents a significant expense for them (Anderson, 2008, Better Regulation Executive, 2009); accurate guidance reduces the uncertainties and the cost.

> Apply to your work
>
> What range of guidance do you provide? Do you supply copies of standards or should regulatees provide their own?

Licensing or Registration

In some regulatory frameworks, those who wish to trade in the sector need to register or obtain a licence. Licensing or registration bodies screen applicants before granting a 'license to trade' and this screening is normally in the form of an assessment of the ability of the applicant to comply with the legal or accreditation requirements. The process would usually look at professional expertise, business viability and personal and corporate histories but, of course, this will vary with the regulatory body. Licensing and registration brings with it the applicant's acceptance and implementation of obligations and responsibilities embedded in the specific sector legislation, contractual or accreditation/certification framework.

Not all organisations are required to licence or register. In particular, health and safety legislation are immediately applicable to employers and in some cases employees and subcontractors (Johnstone et al., 2005). The key phrase here is 'duty holder' – who, within the organization, is a duty holder under the specific legislation. It is this duty holder who should expect contact from a regulator.

Legislation, Regulations and Standards

This section is an overview of the legislative background to regulation as readers may be in differing legal systems.

Primary and Secondary Legislation

Figure 5: Primary and Secondary Legislation

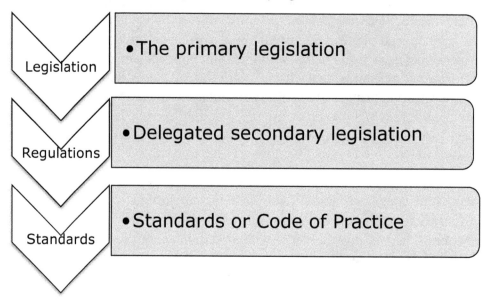

For government regulators, primary legislation gives the scope, powers, purpose, principles and detail of their work. The legislative body, congress or parliament, passes primary legislation. However, often the primary legislation may be fairly broad and vague. In order to make these more specific, and so that those who are inspected can also comprehend and prepare, the primary legislation delegates power to 'another', it could be the regulator or a minister of state, to create secondary legislation providing more specific detail referred to as 'the regulations'. These are either a set of distinct rules or guidelines compiled into a Code of Practice, often with guidance.

Secondary or delegated legislation has the same power as primary statute – it must be obeyed. Standards derive from the regulations but also draw on associated legislation and on the objectives of the regulator.

Before we move on to standards you may wish to look at your own legislation. Both types of legislation (primary and secondary) set out the duties of the regulator - things they *must* do - and their powers - things they *may* do if they deem them appropriate.

> Apply to your work
>
> If you are in a governmental regulatory body, try reading the original legislation that brought the regulatory organisation into being and describes its duties and powers. For those using private and civil standards, identify the source documents for the standards used.

Standards

Standards are arguably the most important tool used by regulators. A standard is a statement of what the regulated establishment should do or aspire to do (Scott, 2010). They provide a means of measuring and evaluating the performance of an organisation by looking at:

- The evidence that the standard requires and then
- Contrast with evidence of how the organisation is working.

Standards set by state regulators differ from private-sector standards. The essential differences are set out below.

Standards Drawn from Private Enterprise and Civil Bodies

- They are recommendations, not legal requirements
- Their use is voluntary BUT must be adhered to if accreditation and membership of a private standards body is to be maintained
- They are available to the public
- They are established by the consensus of all parties concerned
- They are based on the consolidated results of science, technology and experience
- They are approved and published by a recognised standards or civil body.

Standards Drawn from Legislation

- Usually backed by the force of law, they must be met to the satisfaction of the regulator
- They are available to the public
- They may prescribe processes directly or by reference to a private set of third-party standards thus making those standards legally enforceable
- They are adopted by an authority (European Committee for Standardization, 2005).

How Are Standards Created?

There are a number of methods for developing standards. They can be based on or incorporate a regulation. In some instances the legislation will provide the standards with a legal status, using phrases such as 'the standards must be taken into account' or 'the standards have the full force of law'. Some authorities, such as Scotland's National Care Standards Committee, have the legislative power to create standards.

Standards Created by Private Organisations

Private organisations may create, of course, their own sets of standards. ISO produces private standards, as does the European Framework for Quality Management (EFQM), the American National Standards Institute (ANSI) and the Standardization Administration of the People's Republic of China (SAC) (see Scott, 2010). Such standards are international – Busch (2004) describes their use as 'transforming' global agriculture and food trade. International standards on qualities of food and grades enable supermarkets to source foodstuffs from many different countries.

Many private-enterprise standards contain significant technical detail. For example, standards in the oil industry will include specification for storage vessels. Other private standards may not be technical but are prescriptive, instructing the organisation as to how it must perform and the way in which it must do so. An example is this ISO standard for a quality manual:

The organization shall establish and maintain a quality manual that includes a) the scope of the quality management system including details of and justification for any exclusions b) the documented procedures established for the quality management system, or reference to them, and c) a description of the interaction between the processes of the quality management system (ISO Central Secretariat, 2008: p. 57).

There are also private standards, created by civil bodies such as the Forest Stewardship Council for example, that intertwine with government and business regulation (Bartley and Smith, 2010).

Variations and Hybrids

A variation of the above is a government regulator that incorporates private standards, such as ISO, into their legislated standards framework. For example, the US Food and Drug Administration Agency created Quality System 820 for medical device manufacturers, which is harmonized with ISO 9001. The reason for this is that manufacturers prefer to use internationally-recognised standards in order to facilitate global sales, manufacture and supply.

There are also hybrids. In the case of Building Energy Certification, certifying the energy effectiveness of a building in the Republic of Ireland, an EC Directive was transposed into Irish Law which allowed for the inspection, reporting and issuing of building energy certificates (European Parliament and the Council, 2010). Those who inspect buildings and assess the energy rating may, according to the Directive, be self-employed or part of a state agency. Therefore, in some EU countries, building or home inspectors may be employed by the state and, in others, self-employed or employed by a private organisation.

> Apply to your work
>
> Looking at your own organisation, what is the relationship of the standards you use to legislation? Are the standards you use legally enforceable or do they rely on voluntary compliance?

How are Standards Useful?

A standard is a statement of what an organization should do or aspire to do:

- Standards help judge performance and measure the level of compliance - this requires sufficient and detailed data
- Ensuring compliance through the measurement of standards will require enforcement on occasion, but this is likely to be infrequent due to the cost and disruption to the service or business and those who rely upon it (Baldwin et al., 2012: p. 301)
- Standards help make comparisons between providers. The publicised differences in performance help incentivise the provider and the sector towards higher attainment
- Globalised trade is dependent on international standards, usually non-state, to assure providers and purchasers of quality, ethical and technical specification (Busch, 2011).

Standards encourage self-enforced compliance but providers need to know what is required of them. Failure to communicate such information results in sub-standard outcomes despite goodwill on both sides. Self-enforced compliance is a preferred strategy as improvement, perhaps excellence, is much more likely if the provider is working with rather than against the regulator. Regulators, auditors and accreditors have considerable powers with which to implement and persuade compliance with standards and the legislation.

The Powers of the Regulator

Where the regulator works for a state regulatory body, legislation may also determine the powers that regulators can use, for example, the power of entry. It is worth mentioning that such powers make the impersonation of an inspector, for the purposes of fraud, an increasingly common practice (Blanc, 2012). Consequently, validating identity and organisation should always be the first step in contact with establishments.

Regulatory powers vary across legislations, countries and sectors but they consistently provide the power to:

- Inspect any service within the remit of your authority
- Require the organisation to supply relevant information
- At any time, enter and inspect premises
- Inspect and take copies of records, data or documents
- Under certain circumstances, the regulator may seize and remove relevant documents, materials or items and take measurements and photos as evidence
- A regulator is often entitled to have access to any computer used to store relevant records/documents.

You should bear these considerable powers in mind as you plan and begin the regulation visit.

Standards and Systems Theory

Systems Theory clarifies the use and purpose of standards by focussing on the *outcomes* of the organisation (Donabedian, 1980). We define an outcome as follows.

The impact or consequence of a particular service or product.

It is usual to identify the end-user or the customer as experiencing the outcome.

Figure 6: The Systems Model

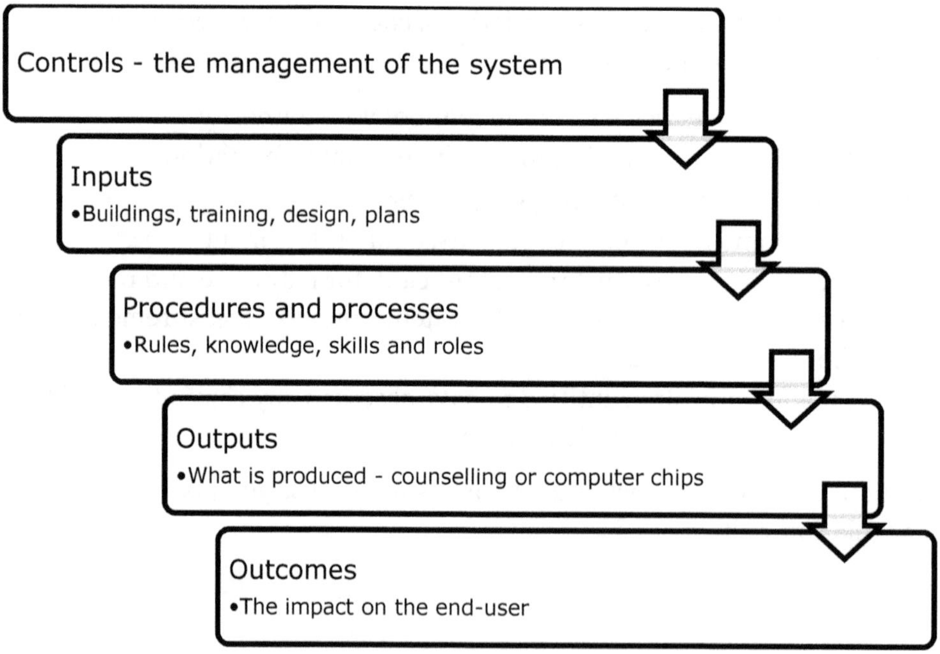

The elements of Systems Theory are:

Inputs – resources, people, skills and the planning necessary to establish the system. This would include resources such as staffing, funding, equipment, buildings and training.

Processes - the means by which inputs become outputs, e.g. the cooking of food. There are many processes but we can talk about one overarching linking process.

Procedures (also known as Protocols) - the documented 'maps' of a process. There will be a series of Standard Operating Procedures (SOPs).

They link to management controls regarding risk and quality. For example, SOPs may direct that you wear a hairnet and gloves when preparing food for retail sale.

Outputs - what the organisation produces. A restaurant has the **output** of a meal but the **outcome** is the impact of the meal on the consumer.

Outcomes – the impact of the output on the citizen, end-user or consumer - should include intended and unintended consequences.

Controls –refers to methods used by management to monitor and change the system based on information received from inside and outside the system. This includes the management of risk, safety and quality.

> Apply to your Work
>
> Can you apply systems theory to your own sector? Look again at the elements on the list above and find the corresponding element in a typical organisation in your sector.

There is a danger of confusing outputs (what is produced) with outcomes (the impact of what is produced) and assuming that because outputs are favourable, the outcome will be favourable. Where a patient is receiving counselling (the output), for example, it does not necessarily follow that they value the experience (the outcome) positively. Outcomes need measuring separately from outputs by collecting information from end-users. The strengths of the systems approach are as follows:

- It gives you the opportunity to look at the organisation in your sector as a set of dynamic processes that contribute to impacts on the end-user
- Processes contribute to outputs and outcomes but they may contain risks
- There are many processes and how they work together is as important as how they work individually; communication between the parts of the system is essential. For example, there may be excellent home care provided for a 77 year old widow after a hip replacement but no-one is delegated to tell her it has been arranged, what form it takes or when it will arrive (author personal communication)
- Systems analysis examines unintended as well as intended outcomes and pinpoints the location of problems.

Regulation as a System

Now that you are familiar with systems theory, we can apply it to regulation as a system. The customer, consumer or citizen is the end-user of regulation. It can be argued that the regulated firm is also a customer as they might pay a fee to the regulator and have a legitimate expectation of a timely and appropriate service. You need to know who your end-user is.

> Apply to your work
>
> Who is the end-user for your work? What is the impact of your service and what is the desired outcome for the end-user?

Outcomes are the impact upon the end-user of the regulatory service. The impact can result in intended or unintended outcomes and can be of a short, medium or long term duration.

An intended outcome is that recognised risks are mitigated and end-users are protected. However, an unintended outcome might be that those hazards and risks not included in the risk-formula are free to impact on the end-user, as seen in the 2007-9 financial crisis - new financial products in international transactions remained outside the regulatory remit with devastating consequences (Black, 2012, Braithwaite, 2015).

Types of Standards

Types of standards correspond to the different elements of a system (Baldwin et al., 2012: Chapter 14) shown below.

Figure 7: Rules-based and Flexible Standards

Rules-based Standards	• Input standards • Process standards

Flexible Standards	• Output standards • Outcome standards • Principle-based standards • Management-based standards

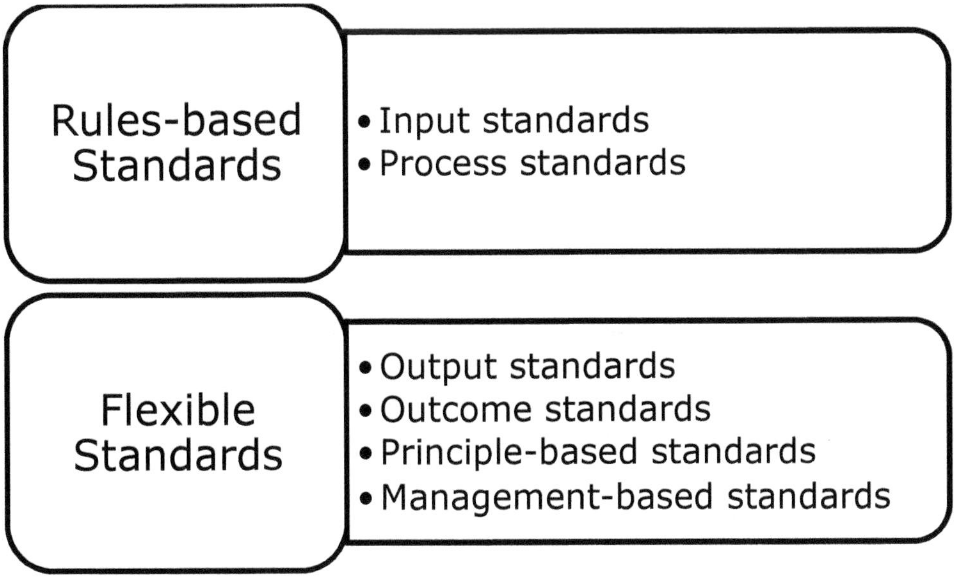

Rules-based standards and flexible standards are very different from one another and foster different regulatory responses:

- Rules-based standards check that specific rules have been met
- Flexible standards audit whether the regulated organisation has the management systems *and* relevant rules to comply with broad flexible standards. The regulator judges whether those flexible standards have been met.

Rules-based Standards

These are, as the name suggests, rules that must be followed to the specification set down. They are 'prescriptive' – they stipulate what must be done or not done.

Input or Design Standards

These specify the resources, skills and other inputs that should be present in the organisation's system. They prescribe specific equipment or may have a scientific specification (Moore et al., 2011)

Process Standards

These are a further type of rules-based standard and specify the process that must be used, for example, two-person labelling of genetic materials to avoid mislabelling. They too are prescriptive standards.

Regulators may have many hundreds of rules-based standards to check. Jin, in researching Florida restaurants, found that inspectors had more than one thousand rules to check (Jin and Lee, 2013).

Flexible Standards

In contrast, flexible standards encourage a firm or institution to look for the solutions and rules that are right for them, presenting their own plan for compliance to the regulator for approval. In this way, they offer new liberty to the regulated, minimizing costs (Bennear and Coglianese, 2012) and offering the flexibility to rapidly accommodate advances in technology. They are also thought to promote a more competitive market by encouraging firms to seek better value and more effective solutions (May, 2003).

Output Standards

These specify a certain level of delivery, for example measured emission levels or product specification, rather than the process used to deliver it. Unlike process standards, output standards leave the producer to decide on the most effective process to use.

Outcome Standards

These standards can be expressed in quantitative or qualitative terms.

The outcome-based approach focuses regulatory attention on the achievement of regulatory objectives rather than carrying out prescribed actions. The ability of regulated entities to choose how to achieve those results provides greater flexibility and opens up possibilities for more cost-effective compliance solutions (May, 2011: p.2).

To achieve this, an outcome measure should be set and the regulator has to be able to measure this. These standards may be specific about the outcome they desire, as in air pollution, or they can be broad, as in this child nursery standard:

> Each child or young person can experience and choose from a balanced range of activities (Scottish Government, 2005).

The regulator and regulated, trade association or civil group, agree the means by which the outcome standard will be met and there may be additional regulatory body guidance.

Principle-based Standards

> Instead of a set of rules, the regulator requires the organisation to meet a broad principle, outlining regulatory values and objectives thus allowing the organisation to choose its own means of complying with the principle without having to follow a set of prescriptive rules (Baldwin et al., 2012: p. 302).

Braithwaite and Braithwaite (1995) contrasted the regulation of care homes comparing Australian broad standards, such as that the care home should be 'homelike', to the US preference for rules governing specific details of the care environment. The perhaps surprising conclusion was that the broad Australian standards promoted creativity and quality in the care environment - managers and staff were released from having to follow prescriptive rules to the letter. Principle-based standards are not 'tick-box' – there must be a professional *judgement* made on whether the principle has been achieved. An example of a principle-based standard is taken from UK financial regulation:

> A firm must pay due regard to the interests of its customers and treat them fairly (Financial Conduct Authority, 2015).

A broad principle such as this may have substantial guidance and prescriptive rules but, in some situations, the regulatee has considerable freedom to meet the principle in a way they find most suitable.

Management-based Standards

The final type of flexible standard stipulates that the firm has a quality-management or risk-management system or both. This type of requirement is found across the USA, Australia and Europe. The best-known example is the Hazard and Critical Control Point (HACCP) systems required by most food-safety regulators. The organisation manufacturing, supplying or selling food has to show that it has in place a system that controls the risks and hazards that may arise (International HACCP Alliance, 2015). There is detailed guidance and close monitoring.

The Problems with Flexible Standards

It is not an either/or choice between flexible standards and rules-based standards - they both have advantages and disadvantages. We have mentioned some of the drawbacks of rules-based/prescriptive standards:

- They don't keep up with change
- They are inflexible
- They produce a violation-seeking form of inspection or audit
- They stifle innovation.

However, flexible standards are implicated in a number of disasters and failures (Black, 2014, Black, 2010a, Braithwaite, 2015, Coglianese, 2015).

One such example is the Pike River Coal Mine Tragedy, New Zealand. In 2010, there was an explosion of methane gas at Pike River Coal Mine and 29 miners lost their lives, 13 of whom were sub-contracted workers. The consequent report found many reasons for the tragedy but regulatory strategies were significant.

The health and safety legislation of New Zealand had adopted outcomes-based standards, expressed at a high level, but this did not include the codes of practice or regulations to support the mine managements' health and safety system. Additionally, the regulator had only two inspectors to cover mining over the whole of New Zealand and they were not trained in quality or safety-system audit. The management of the mine had implemented neither a sound safety system nor the necessary equipment or practices. Workforce training was haphazard and the contractors had neither their own safety systems nor training in the Pike River Mine health and safety systems (Lamare et al., 2015). There was no culture of safety and management were slow to make improvements, many of which had been suggested by the workers. The report commented:

---

the necessary support for the legislation, through detailed regulations and codes of practice, did not appear. Instead, the opposite happened: such regulations as existed were repealed when the HSE Act came into force. The special rules and safeguards applicable to mining contained in the old law, based on many years of hard-won experience from past tragedies, were swept away by the new legislation, leaving mining operators and the mining inspectors in limbo (Royal Commission on the Pike River Coal Mine Tragedy, 2012: p. 32).

The Balance between Flexibility and Accountability

Flexible standards confront a fundamental regulatory issue and that is how the regulator can maintain control and consistency without stifling efficiency and innovation. What the Pike River disaster demonstrates is that there is a balance between flexibility and innovation and accountability and that specific rules help both regulators and the regulated in managing quality and health and safety systems (May, 2003).

Dialogue with the organisation is necessary to decide the codes and rules needed to support the flexible standard; some firms may not be capable of this because they lack the skills and the resources. Where trust is limited and the skills necessary are not apparent, a reliance on rules-based standards is preferable, or a mix of the two:

> ... outcomes focused regulation places significant demands on both regulators and regulatees' judgement and expertise. However, complex systems of detailed rules can be just as demanding to implement and have the additional disadvantage of becoming easily outdated, as in the case of the regulatory regime for deep water drilling in the US. Th(is) ... highlights the care that has to be taken in designing a rules-based system, to ensure there is the right combination of principles or outcomes-focused norms and sufficient 'scaffolding' through more detailed guidance provisions to indicate to firms how to comply, and assure themselves and regulators that they have done so (Black, 2014: p. 13).

Trust is an important factor in the success of flexible standards. Organisations and individuals have to be trusted to implement fully the agreed regime but the regulator must also be vigilant in monitoring the implementation.

In some cases, trust is misplaced. This was the case with the Volkswagen emissions scandal in 2015. VW eventually admitted that there was software installed in their diesel engines that reduced emissions when it sensed the car was being tested (Coglianese, 2015). However, when the car was driven normally emissions were up to 35 times greater than the regulatory limit (an output standard), the software was illegal and the deception had been ongoing since 2009.

Standards and Grading

There is consistent support for the argument that compliance with standards is one way in which a regulator can contribute to the improvement of a service or product (Brennan, 1998, Jones and Tymms, 2014). This process is developed further through star ratings or gradings of the standards. These gradings are arrived at:

- Through a formula, for example using the number of violations (Ho, 2012)
- Using the number of stated features present in a checklist
- By using an A, B, C, and D or traffic light colour system
- By using words and terms such as 'inadequate', 'needs improvement', 'good' and 'excellent'.

Motivation and Grading

Grading is a form of disclosure often performed through a workplace regulation visit and then made public either through a website or by putting the 'score on the door'. The most widespread example has been the grading of quality and safety in restaurants and fast food establishments (FSA, 2009, Ho, 2012, Jin and Lee, 2012, Jin and Lee, 2010, Jin and Lee, 2013, Jones et al., 2004, Ryan and Detsky, 2015).

Grading and other forms of ratings schemes are designed to change consumer preferences and, in so doing, it is assumed that grading will also positively affect the motivation of management to improve the product or service.

Grading – Could do Better

On balance, grading is seen as effective but not without its problems (Ho, 2012, Jin and Leslie, 2009). Ho makes these comments on grading schemes in the US:

- Regulatory bodies should release detailed data on the scheme they run in order that others may evaluate it
- This wholesale release of data should then be used by commercial public rating sites such as Yelp or Trip Advisor rather than relying

on regulatory body sites which are not as popular with the public (see also FSA, 2009)

- Inspection criteria should be simplified to reduce variability across regulators
- Regulator visits should be at random intervals. (Ho, 2012: p. 650-657).

New Skills

Flexible standards require skill-sets different from those used for rules-based standards (Gunningham, 2012). These skills include:

- The ability to monitor if an outcome or principles-based standard has been achieved
- The ability to mediate on a firm's interpretation of a principle
- The ability to audit a quality and risk-management system
- An understanding of quality management and risk-based approaches to regulation
- The ability to gauge when and how much to trust the regulated body
- Greater reliance on the professional judgement of the regulator.

Skill in risk-assessment and management is essential and the subject of the next chapter.

Chapter Three: Regulators and Risk

Objectives

After reading this Chapter you will be able to:

- Recognise the different definitions of risk
- Account for the rise of risk-based regulation
- Identify a range of methods for assessing and managing risk
- Ascertain the risks within your sector and determine how businesses and agencies manage these
- Understand the role of Enterprise Risk Management (ERM) models in your work
- Recognise appropriate models of risk-regulation for your sector.

Rationale

The regulation of risk is not new. Medieval market regulations and rules banning gunpowder factories from towns reveal that regulation has always dealt with risk. In fact, most standards exist to prevent a risk:

> The primary rationale justifying many regulatory activities is the reduction of risk to the public (Paoli and Wiles, 2015: p. 13).

This chapter examines a range of concepts and tools relevant to the regulation of risk. There is no one definition of risk. There is no single methodology to apply to risk. Welcome to the risk chapter.

Introduction

> There is no agreed definition of the concept of risk. If we study the literature we find a number of different ways of understanding the risk concept. Some definitions are based on probability, chance or expected values, some on undesirable events or danger, and others on uncertainties (Aven, 2012: p. 33).

We should not despair at the absence of an agreed definition. Rather, lack of agreement offers the opportunity to focus on the different facets of risk encountered by front-line regulators.

Regulators scrutinise whether organisations are effectively managing the risks they produce and whether the public are gaining a benefit:

> Conducting a risk-based inspection requires inspectors to focus their efforts on evaluating the degree of active managerial control that operators have over ... risk factors (USFDA, 2013: p. 494).

Front line regulators investigate 'active managerial control over risk factors'. This chapter sets out areas relevant to that task:

- Concepts of risk-management and risk-assessment processes and how they involve business, government and civic society in serving the public interest
- A review of possibly the most frequently-encountered risk tool, the risk-matrix
- Designed for business, Enterprise Risk Management (ERM) adopts a different definition of risk and draws on the knowledge base of audit. This different perspective is essential knowledge for regulators involved with business audit and corporate governance models
- A range of risk tools are introduced explaining how, why and when organisations might apply them
- Finally, we look at the tensions between the major definitions of risk and regulating in the public interest.

Risk-based Regulation

Regulators are increasingly accountable for their management of business and professional risk-taking (Black, 2010b). Risk is arguably the major justification for regulation and, by implication, the fundamental role of inspectors and auditors is to assess and manage risks posed by the organisations and sectors they regulate.

The financial crisis of 2007-9 underlines the effects of inadequate risk-management by regulatory bodies across the globe:

> failures by regulators to monitor individual financial institutions or individuals and/or failure to challenge firms when failures were identified, through lack of skills, resources, resolve and/or political support; and failure to anticipate or understand the endogenous effects of regulation itself, including the role of moral hazard in shaping market behaviour (Black, 2011: p. 1 citing FSA 2009).

The increasing dominance of a risk-based approach to regulation is attributed to:

- The belief that the role of regulation is to prevent and/or reduce the harm produced through natural hazards, business, science, organisations and individuals
- The notion that regulation can improve risk-management in a sector and particularly in those firms that produce the highest risks
- The requirement for regulatory bodies to demonstrate that organisations are being regulated proportionate to the risks they produce
- The desire to comply with legislation requiring risk-regulation (Black, 2010a: p. 189).

The Risk-management Process

Risk-assessment and risk-management are two parts of a process referred to as risk governance. The risk-governance process shown below is adapted from Renn and Graham (2006: p. 13).

Figure 8: Risk Governance: Risk-assessment and Risk-management

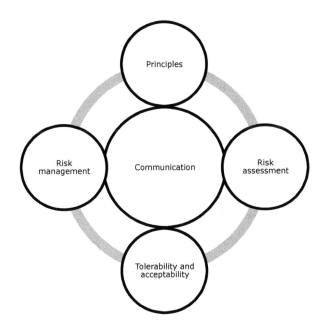

The process is explained below.

Principles

Risk governance is an approach to risk-assessment and risk-management that includes dialogue with all stakeholders as well as scientific and statistical methods. Its principles are:

- Communication
- Inclusion
- Integration
- Reflection.

Communication must be two-way and continuous and is central to the process, not a separate stage. It goes beyond information and education, 'communication and trust are delicately interconnected' (Van Asselt and Renn, 2011: p. 440). It involves civil society, consumers, experts, business, regulators and government.

Inclusion may include forums, advisory committees, consensus building and conflict resolution. Inclusion does not just mean that stakeholders are included but that they have a significant role in defining risk.

The **Integration** principle promotes the collecting and interpreting of relevant facts, knowledge, perceptions and values from divergent stakeholders. Where there are uncertain risks, the application of probability and measurability will only give a partial picture.

Reflection - Time should be set aside, within the process, to reflect on and reconsider the difficult decisions to be made.

Risk-assessment

Four questions capture the risk-assessment process:

- What can go wrong?
- What is the likelihood?
- What are the consequences?
- Over what time frame (Haimes, 2009: p. 1651)?

Risk is an intrinsic part of modern business and scientific culture. For example, the aviation industry seeks to minimise risks whilst the banking industry calculates the maximum risk it is prepared to work with (Ashby et al., 2012). In both cases, risk-analysis involves estimating when taking a risk may have a harmful or have a beneficial impact. Risk is not only discernible in business, it is a notion we all use – for example, we allow our children to take risks in order to develop both physically and socially (the playground and the playing field).

The definition of risk below embraces such wider human values as well as the notion of loss and optimal gain:

> Risk is a situation or event where something of human value (including humans themselves) is at stake and where the outcome is uncertain (Rosa, 1998: p. 28).

This definition captures four features of risk:

1. Risk expresses human concern or interest
2. An outcome is possible and can occur
3. There is uncertainty about the possible impacts
4. The outcomes may be harmful or beneficial.

The final point makes clear that a risk definition is not only concerned with adverse events but also in taking opportunities where the benefits outweigh the risks.

Apply to your work

Compare the risks you regulate in your sector with the definition given above by Rosa.

Is the risk of human concern?

Is there uncertainty about the potential consequences? Are the outcomes harmful or beneficial?

Figure 9: The Boulder May Dislodge (adapted from Aven et al., 2011: p. 1075)

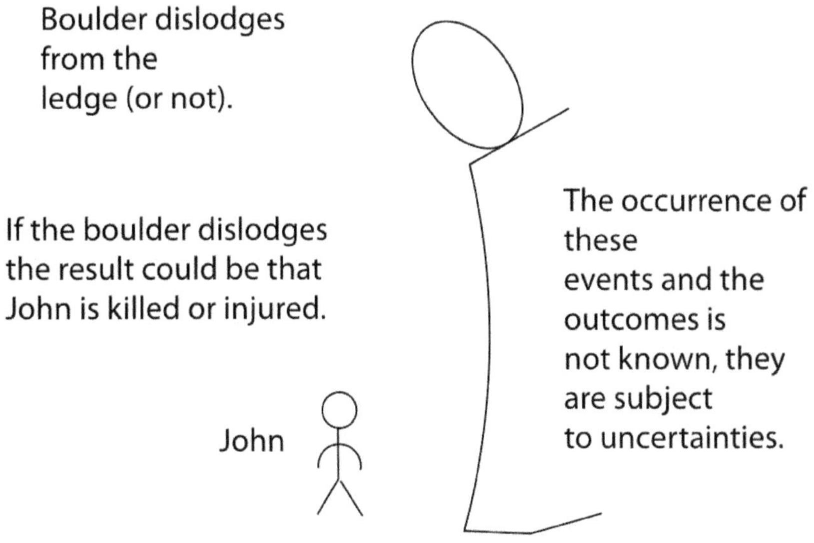

Boulder dislodges from the ledge (or not).

If the boulder dislodges the result could be that John is killed or injured.

The occurrence of these events and the outcomes is not known, they are subject to uncertainties.

John

To illustrate Rosa's definition and what is meant by uncertainty, we can take the case of John and the boulder, illustrated above. John is walking under a cliff with a boulder perched precariously on the cliff top. Whether the boulder will dislodge is subject to uncertainty. If the boulder does fall, with any luck, it will miss John. On the other hand, it may kill or maim him. The consequence of the boulder falling is uncertain. That John is completely unaware of the boulder does not affect the risk.

The example illustrates the difficulties of trying to estimate a risk situation when outcomes and the event itself are uncertain. As with the boulder example, many risks are difficult to estimate, motivating the International Risk Governance Council (IRGC) to put forward four categories to describe risks:

Table 1: Categories of Risk (Renn and Graham, 2006: p. 12)

	Examples of Category
Simple	Known health risks, such as those related to smoking
Complex	The failure risk of interconnected technical systems, such as the electricity transmission grid
Uncertain	Atrocities, such as those resulting from the changed nature and scale of international terrorism
Ambiguous	The long-term effects and ethical acceptability of controversial technologies, such as nanotechnology.

The categories reflect the diversity of risk hazards and expose the enduring challenges of risk-assessment and risk-management:

- Is there evidence of a cause-and-effect relationship between the event and the consequences?
- Do the anticipated consequences take into account the views of those directly affected?
- What values are used in deciding what is to be done and what is acceptable?

> Apply to your work
>
> Are there examples in your work of the four categories of risk described above?

Even in the case of simple categories of risk, there may be complex factors that prevent a solution. For example, the relationship between trans-fat in food and heart disease has been known for some time but opposition by vested interests can delay a risk-management solution for many years (Graham and Noe, 2015: p. 6-7).

With the Uncertain and Ambiguous categories, there is a lack of quantitative data and knowledge. Probability calculations are of limited value if when the event will occur, or what its likely consequence will be, is unknown.

Nevertheless, not everything is uncertain. Quantitative and qualitative data, where they are available and relevant, are important for risk-assessment and risk-management, consequently there are a wide range of tools and techniques available.

Quantitative Risk-assessments derive from statistical analysis of large data sets, employed to increase knowledge of a particular risk event, source or hazard by:

- Collection of statistical data relating to the **performance** of a risk source in the past (actuarial extrapolation)
- Collection of statistical data relating to **components** of a hazardous agent or technology. This method requires a synthesis of probability judgements from component failure to system performance (probabilistic risk assessments, PRA)
- Epidemiological or experimental studies, which are aimed at finding **statistically significant correlations** between an exposure of a hazardous agent and an adverse effect in a defined population sample (probabilistic modelling) (Renn and Graham, 2006: p. 27).

Advantages – based on objective analysis rather than subjectivity.

Disadvantages – large samples and data sets are necessary to show correlation that often makes these prohibitively expensive. Using small samples and low quality data may be unreliable.

Qualitative-assessments of risk are necessary where the risk is Complex, Uncertain and Ambiguous and little quantitative information is available. This process includes:

- Conflict-resolution
- Local intelligence and whistleblowing
- Stakeholder involvement
- Emphasis on communication

- Experts, or decision makers best estimates of probabilities, in particular for events where only insufficient statistical data is available
- Scenario techniques by which different plausible pathways from release of a harmful agent to the final loss are modelled on the basis of worst and best cases or estimated likelihood for each consequence (Renn and Graham, 2006: p. 27).

Advantages – expert judgements are able to capture wisdom and experience that is unsuited to quantitative analysis.

Disadvantages – solutions lack wide acceptance without the involvement of all stakeholders.

Hybrid System – most assessments use a combination of both qualitative and quantitative assessment (Blanc, 2012):

Trying to assess risk is therefore necessarily a social and political exercise, even when the methods employed are the seemingly technical routines of quantitative risk assessments ... regulation calls for a more open-ended process, with multiple access points for dissenting views and unorthodox perspectives... (Jasanoff, 1999 cited in Aven and Renn, 2009: p. 6).

It is important to understand the perceptions held concerning risk (risk perception) and the estimates of social, physical and economic impacts. Figure 10 illustrates the transition from risk perception, to risk-assessment to risk-management.

Figure 10: The Risk-assessment/management Process. Reprinted with permission of ScienceCartoonsPlus.com

Acceptability and Tolerability of Risk

The most difficult decisions of the risk-management process involve deciding when risks are intolerable, tolerable and acceptable:

- **Intolerable** risks exist where the hazard, such as use of a chemical or medicine, should be abandoned, transferred or replaced. If that is not possible, then vulnerability and exposure should be reduced. This could be achieved through education, regulation, standards or minimising use.
- **Tolerable** risks exist where the harms of exposure to the risk are outweighed by the benefits. This requires reduction of the risk through risk-management.
- **Acceptable** risks are those deemed so negligible that significant risk-management is not required.

As can be imagined, in situations where there are opposing views on the risks and/or conflicting or weak data, it becomes difficult to reach consensus.

Figure 11: Acceptable, Tolerable and Intolerable Risks (adapted from Renn and Graham, 2006: p. 37)

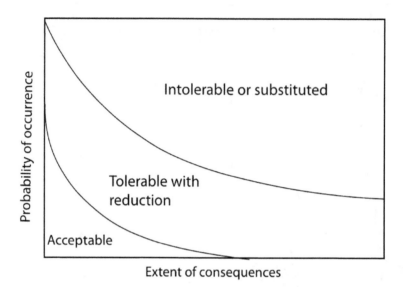

Risk-management

Risk-management is a process of controlling and reducing risks using the following tools:

- Technical standards and limits that prescribe the permissible threshold of concentrations, emissions, take-up or other measures of exposure
- Performance standards for technological and chemical processes such as minimum temperature limits in waste incinerators
- Technical prescriptions referring to the blockage of exposure (e.g. via protective clothing) or the improvement of resilience (e.g. via immunisation or earthquake tolerant constructions)
- Governmental economic incentives including taxation, duties, subsidies and certification schemes
- Third party incentives, i.e. private monetary or in kind incentives
- Compensation schemes (monetary or in kind)

- Insurance and liability
- Co-operative and informative options ranging from voluntary agreements to labelling, and
- Education programs (Renn and Graham, 2006: p. 42).

There may be interactions with a number of risk-management organisations that function to reduce risk:

inspections by insurance providers, third-party certification schemes, audits by influential customers, and substantial industry self-interest in reputation and brand equity (Paoli and Wiles, 2015: p. 14).

Figure 12 illustrates types of risk-management measures that may be applied. Risk-prevention measures are used prior to an event, accident or malfunction. After an event, preventative and responsive measures to reduce impact are applied.

Figure 12: Prevention and Reaction Strategies (Renn and Graham, 2006: p.21)

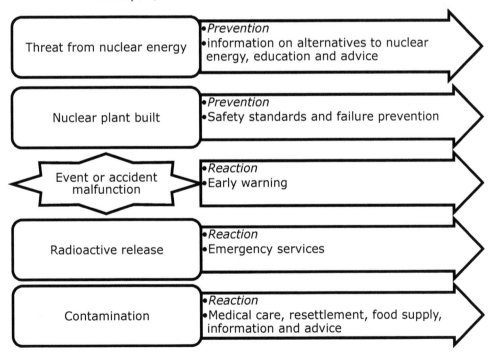

The centre box in Figure 12 represents an accident or malfunction in a nuclear energy plant. Note that risk communication measures include education and information. Standards are a form of risk-prevention. Many regulatory bodies provide information and education as part of risk-management.

On the right are the reactive measures to the accident or malfunction. These include early warning and direct measures to reduce the threat followed by emergency services and continuing medical care and resettlement for those affected.

Flexibility in Risk-regulation

Human actions that are careless, deceptive or just ignorant amplify the uncertainty and ambiguity of risk. Sparrow (Sparrow, 2008) makes the point that rogue traders, sex offenders – or criminals of all types – can deliberately change their strategies of deception to take account of any risk-prevention measures that have been put in place.

Unintentional actions may also heighten risk. If risk-management in an organization is weak or poorly implemented, then individual and organisational ignorance, misunderstanding or incompetence can negate risk measures as we saw in the Pike River Mine tragedy and in the Buncefield Incident (see page 55).

The Risk Matrix

The process of risk-assessment and management (risk governance) is complex and involves multiple stakeholders with divergent views. In contrast, what many frontline regulators will encounter is the risk matrix. This is a simple tool. It is used to show risk tolerance and/or risk prioritisation of (generally adverse) events (Duijm, 2015: p. 21).

The risk-matrix assumes that the probability of an event occurring and its outcome are known and can be calculated. Risk equals:

- The probability of a harmful consequence occurring

Multiplied by

- The severity or consequence of the harm predicted (for a certain group, individual or event).

This is less a definition and more a description of the calculation used.

Scales of probability and severity of consequence are the foundation of risk matrices. There are two axes – probability and consequence. The probability axis often takes the form of a percentage probability but can also use time as in the example below.

The consequence axis may refer to harm or severity or use other ways of qualitatively defining the consequence, such as disaster, for example. The axes may also use a monetary value to indicate the impact of the consequence.

Table 2: Illustrating Axes of Scales and Categories

Probability	Severity of Consequence		
	Low = 1	Medium = 2	High = 3
In the next year =1			
Next 3 months = 2			
Imminent = 3			

In most instances, the risk matrix is used for subjective assessments of probability and consequence and that is its strength. Through interpretation of the probability and consequence categories, people with a minimum of training can reach a risk decision. If the descriptive categories are accurate and consistent, then there is higher possibility of assessor agreement.

The axes may have three classes in each category, as in the example below – three classes of severity and three classes of probability. The fewer the classes, the greater the problem of very different risks scoring in the same box. These are known as 'risk-ties' and are to be avoided. The more classes available the more the differentiation of risk. A popular size is 5 x 5 classes but there can be more or less – too many and the matrix becomes less easy to use.

Multiplying the probability and consequence gives a risk score that can then be mapped on the axes. This mapping is most effective when influencing decision-making regarding risk-priorities and risk-tolerance (what risks you will accept, tolerate or find intolerable).

Table 3: Risk Matrix Showing Prioritisation

Probability	Severity of consequence		
	Low = 1	Medium = 2	High = 3
In the next year =1	1	2	3
Next 3 months = 2	2	4	6
Imminent = 3	3	6	9

In Table 3, the axes produce a numerical value. An event that will occur imminently (=3) and will have a high harmful impact (=3) when multiplied equals a risk score of 9. With this table, it is possible to create a risk tolerance graph as in Figure 11 or a matrix that illustrates the degree of risk-priority as in Table 3. Risk-assessors use the matrix to give a priority to any given unique risk.

Priority bandings assist in risk priority decision-making:

- Scores of 1 and 2 fall into a low-risk band
- Scores of 3 and 4 fall into a medium-risk band
- Scores of 6 or 9 fall into the high-risk band.

Such bandings, also called 'traffic-light' bandings using the colours green, amber and red, are useful for decision-making and resource allocation in a variety of risk situations. The definition and description of the categories and classes is important when assessors are making decisions on risk.

Multiple Hazards

Risk-matrices are not recommended in assessing multiple risks – probability and consequences that individually constitute low risk but, occurring together, can have an extreme impact. This was the case with the Buncefield Incident (Buncefield MIIB, 2008) where a fuel storage depot in the UK exploded, resulting in a fire that lasted for days. Small faults had not been fixed; these low risk events combined to cause a disaster.

What to know about the Risk Matrix

- It communicates priorities and risk-tolerance graphically
- The use of qualitative descriptions in the classes helps to make quick and local decisions on risk factors
- Constructed around one risk dimension (for example, food safety) it encapsulates expert and quantitative knowledge of critical process, scientific knowledge and probability
- It may oversimplify very complex risk hazards and give the appearance of managing the risk
- It may encourage a 'centring bias' where values in the middle are chosen
- It should use additional risk information to support decision making
- A risk matrix designed to cover all the operations of an organization may not be sufficiently specific for the risks encountered (Duijm, 2015, Cox, 2008).

The Business Management of Risk

How firms manage risk has changed dramatically over the past 10 years:

> There is a strong belief that risk management provides the adequate tool for balancing the conflicts inherent in exploring opportunities on the one hand, and avoiding losses, accidents and disasters, on the other. Different standards and frameworks have been developed to effectively identify, assess and manage risk, including the AS/NZS 4360 Risk Management Standard [1] and the ISO 31000 standard on risk-management (Aven, 2011: p. 719).

The financial crisis has been one factor in heightened risk-management. Another has been the belief by the firms themselves that the effective management of risk adds value – it prevents loss and maintains profit (Farrell and Gallagher, 2015).

Enterprise Risk Management (ERM)

Enterprise Risk Management (ERM) systems have been in existence for just over a decade (Farrell and Gallagher, 2015). Central to ERM is the aim of integrating risk-management into all aspects and divisions of the business or organisation. ERM accepts that risk can be harmful but also sees risk-management as an everyday part of business:

> as an interactive process for identifying and assessing those risks that may limit the achievement of enterprise objectives (Moeller, 2013: p. 59).

The objective is *not* to eradicate risk but to maintain it at an acceptable level, referred to as the residual risk. Unlike the previous definition of risk by Rosa (see page 44), ERM schemes focus on the firm's objectives. The ISO 31000 standard on risk-management defines risk as:

> the effect of uncertainty on objectives (ISO, 2009).

Here the effect can be either positive or negative. There is a strong focus on the business and its processes and on the management of those.

The approach may be one with which regulators are unfamiliar. However, ISO, COSO and Australian & New Zealand standards, together with the Cadbury Code on corporate governance, will be the systems of risk-assessment and risk-management that regulators will encounter in the private sector – a good reason to be familiar with them.

Inherent Risk and Residual Risk

Some risks are inherent to industries and enterprises; risks such as metal fatigue cannot be avoided. Such inherent risks may result in harm, loss or injury. The objective of risk-management is to reduce the impact of inherent risk even if you cannot remove it altogether.

Using controls can reduce or remove risk. A control is any procedure, appliance or protocol that functions to lessen or reduce the inherent risk. For example, a guard on a machine reduces the risk of a moving shaft trapping clothing. A range of risk-management controls are illustrated on page 50.

Figure 13: The Residual Risk Equation

It is not possible, as in the case of pipe corrosion in oil refineries, to remove inherent risks entirely but they can be reduced or mitigated. In some cases, a number of controls might be combined to mitigate risk. The Residual Risk refers to the risk of harm that remains after the application of the control(s).

> Apply to your work
>
> What are the inherent risks in your sector? What controls provide an acceptable residual risk?

Controls and Enterprise Risk-management (ERM)

The definition of a 'control' is more wide-ranging than you might think and private sector standards spell it out. For example, the Committee of Sponsoring Organisations of the Treadway Commission (COSO) recognise five forms of control. Intuitively we think of a risk control as one operative checking another's work or levels of training before engaging in a process. However, what are defined as 'controls' embrace the whole organisation from the top to the bottom (see Figure 14).

Figure 14: Controls According To COSO (Mcnally, 2013)

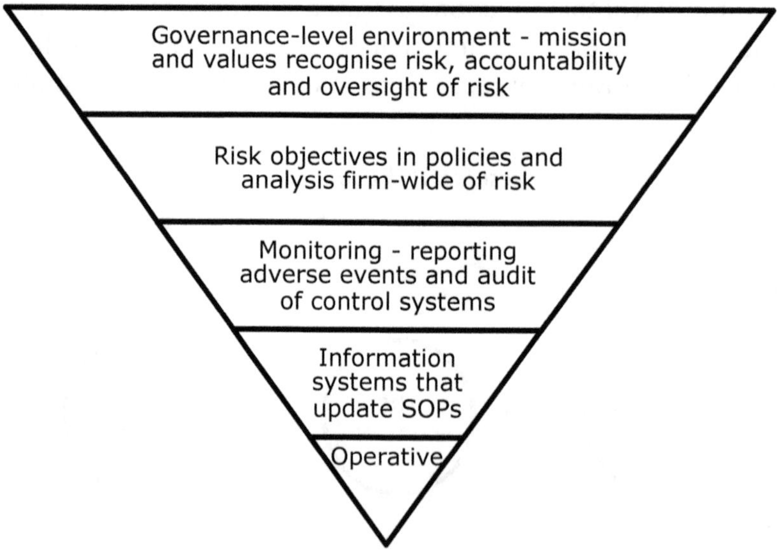

Governance-level environment - mission and values recognise risk, accountability and oversight of risk

Risk objectives in policies and analysis firm-wide of risk

Monitoring - reporting adverse events and audit of control systems

Information systems that update SOPs

Operative

> Apply to your work
>
> Are there Enterprise Risk Management standards in your sector? If so, how do you use them?

Misplaced Emphasis on Controls

Within the ERM framework, controls are working properly if they maintain the residual level. The critical assessment is judged by the degree of risk tolerated at the residual level, not by whether a control is in place or not.

Consequently, inspection and audit are concerned with residual risk-levels, rather than with merely checking whether the control is in place (Coetzee and Lubbe, 2014). In an annual survey of audit practice, it has been emphasised that too many auditors are merely checking that a control is in place rather than assessing if that control is resulting in an acceptable level of residual risk. (Price Waterhouse Cooper, 2014).

In fact, the control, as can be seen from the diagram above, is only one part of successful risk-management; risk policies and practices should be evidenced at every level of the organisation.

Lalonde and Boiral suggest caution in assuming the integrity of a standard such as ISO31000, the COSO framework or AS/NZS 4360. They point to problems with implementation and the lack of independent review in:

- Organizations that develop inadequate risk management systems or do not use them efficiently or properly
- Organizations that are too small and more generally, companies that lack resources to invest in sophisticated risk management system
- Organizations that do not manage to integrate risk management into their organizational work/praxis
- Organizations that adopt risk management system as a rational ritual that provides the company with a false feeling of safety and thereby raises their overall risk level
- Organizations that do not invest in human capital (Lalonde and Boiral, 2012: p. 283).

Given the variance of implementation, it is prudent for regulators to take a critical attitude to claims of having a risk standard in place.

Tools for Managing Risk

Risk-assessment and management uses various tools and perspectives. The following are useful in identifying the **inherent risks** in the workplace.

Process Mapping

When you map a process, such as manufacturing a medical device, for example, you identify all the stages of production. This type of risk-assessment is common in industries with standard operating procedures to control the hazards innate in certain kinds of equipment such as storage vessels. Process mapping establishes the process and puts in place risk prevention and emergency responses. The petroleum and oil industries (API, 2009) and medical processes (Mortimer and Mortimer, 2005) provide examples.

Regulators use process mapping to educate small businesses on the inherent risks of, for example, food production processes, as shown below, and the preventive risk measures or controls that can be implemented.

The UK Food Standards Agency produced the chart (see Figure 15) as part of a larger document on risks and hazards in managing food contamination. Food production businesses can see the relevance of the material and they will know immediately what the regulator requires or recommends.

Figure 15: Process Mapping

Safe method:

Personal hygiene

It is vital for staff to follow good personal hygiene
practices to help prevent bacteria from spreading to food.

Safety point	Why?	How do you do this?
Staff should always wash their hands thoroughly before preparing food. (See the 'Handwashing' method in the Cleaning section.)	Handwashing is one of the best ways to prevent harmful bacteria from spreading.	Are all staff trained to wash their hands before preparing food? Yes ☐ No ☐
All staff should wear clean clothes when working with food. Ideally, they should change into clean work clothes before starting work and not wear these clothes outside food preparation areas.	Clothes can bring dirt and bacteria into food preparation areas. Wearing clean clothes helps to prevent this.	Do your staff wear clean work clothes? Yes ☐ No ☐ Do your staff change clothes before starting work?
Ideally, work clothes should be long-sleeved and light-coloured (to show the dirt) with no external pockets. It is also a good idea to wear a clean apron or disposable apron over work clothes.	This prevents skin from touching food and helps to stop hairs, fibres and the contents of pockets (which can carry bacteria) getting into food.	Yes ☐ No ☐ Describe your staff's work clothes here:

Regulators encourage managers of regulated organisations to develop:

> Their own process and management system standards and
> develop internal planning and management designed to
> achieve (inspection standards) (Gunningham, 2012: p. 7).

Many regulators require that the regulated organisation's own risk-management conforms to set standards. The regulator may set these or expect an ERM to be in place, a procedure known as *management-based regulation* (Coglianese and Lazer, 2003).

Quality Critical Processes

Quality Critical Processes is a technique developed from process mapping by identifying specific parts of the process as high inherent-risk and critical to quality. You might identify these high-risk processes in your regulated sector by asking the following questions:

- Which processes generate most customer complaints?
- Which processes generate most errors?
- Which processes appear unpredictable?
- Which processes contain bottlenecks where a product or service output slows down?

> Apply to your work
>
> How do you assess risks specific to the regulated organisation?

Sharp End - Blunt End: The Role of Human Error

Regulators are often criticised for only detecting hazards but then not looking for the underlying systemic causes (Gunningham, 2012). One example would be to point out a machine operative breaking safety rules without also recognising that the piecework rate on that machine is not achievable without doing so. The regulator corrects the symptoms but not the causes.

Research on human error in organisations (Reason, 1990) provides a model that locates workplace error as part of a systemic breakdown. Known as 'blunt end and sharp end' (see Figure 16) the model demonstrates the linkage between the assumed operator error and weaknesses in systemic control of hazards and risks.

Figure 16: Sharp End Blunt End

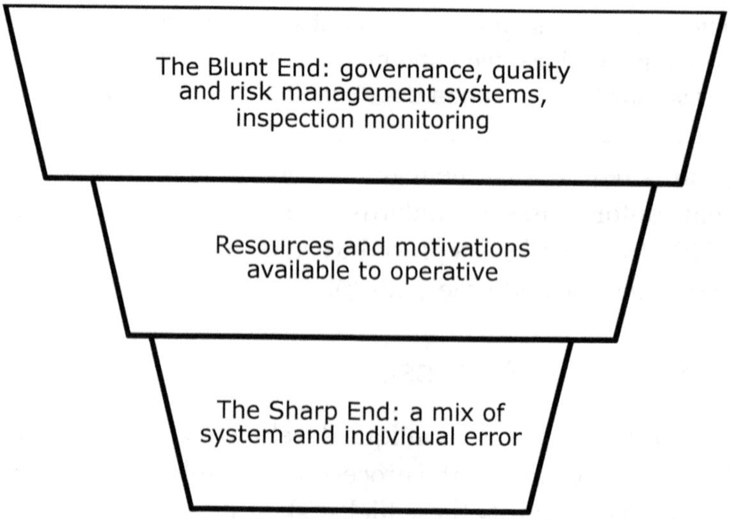

The Blunt End: governance, quality and risk management systems, inspection monitoring

Resources and motivations available to operative

The Sharp End: a mix of system and individual error

For example, when a surgeon leaves a surgical instrument inside a patient, how much is that error due to the incompetence of the surgeon? The blunt end/sharp end model might point to the insufficient resources available such as poor lighting in the surgery, lack of surgical assistance and exhausting workloads.

Making sure that policies and quality and risk-management systems are working properly is a vital element of regulation. You will see in Figure 16 above that the regulator contributes to system error if it fails to monitor the organisation's management of risk and to communicate the findings.

Equally, it is important to emphasise that individuals *do* make decisions that result in hazards outside of what it is possible for management to control i.e. criminality.

Root Cause Analysis – Seeking the Causes of Adverse Events

Root Cause Analysis (RCA) starts with the similar assumption that most adverse events are the results of system and process issues rather than human error. Even where human error has occurred the inference is that the process can be altered in order to prevent human error. RCA however, is concerned with analysing *specific* causes in unique situations.

The most useful definition of a root cause is:

The most basic cause that can be reasonably identified and changed.

The definition contains three key elements:

- *Basic cause* - Specific reasons as to why an incident occurred that enable recommendations that will prevent or reduce recurrence of the events leading up to the incident.
- *Reasonable identification* - There has to be a stop point for the analysis that is within the control of the organisation. Causes could be analysed forever, which would be less than beneficial.
- *Control to fix* - General classifications such as 'operator error' should be avoided. Such causes are not sufficiently specific to allow those in charge to rectify the situation (Livingston et al., 2001: p. 8).

Use of a bank cash machine (ATM) is a good example of how to avoid human error by altering the process. You go to the ATM to get out money and do so by putting in your card and keying in your PIN. When the money is dispensed, which is what you came for, you take the money but forget to take your card out of the machine. Most ATMs now avoid this human error by making it necessary to withdraw your card before you can get your money – leaving your card in the machine is reduced to almost zero.

> Apply to your work
>
> Drawing on your experience, can you identify where human error had, at least in part, a systemic cause?

Recording and Sharing Adverse Events

Several recent serious adverse incidents have attracted high profile national media attention. These include a case of misappropriation of embryos by an errant scientist misleading both patients and colleagues; the loss of a large amount of stored sperm through equipment failure and two cases of mix-up of sperm and embryos – including one that was not recognized until the birth of baby with an incongruous phenotype. Some have said that these incidents are the 'tip of the iceberg', but this comment probably exaggerates the problem. Nevertheless, there is evidence that adverse incidents are significantly under-reported (Kennedy, 2004: p 169).

Some regulators encourage the reporting of adverse events. The UK's Human Fertilisation and Embryology Authority (HFEA), following the series of events outlined above and persuaded by a landmark inquiry that firmly placed risk oversight with the regulator (Toft, 2004), set up a system whereby clinics reported adverse events to them. HFEA would then share the information with all clinics. At first, regulated clinics were cautious in reporting adverse events – it is difficult to own up to something going wrong - but the benefit was recognised. The recording of adverse events contributes to the improvement of quality if circulated amongst other clinics and seen as an opportunity to understand where a process went wrong rather than to lay blame (Toffel and Short, 2011).

Apply to your work

How do you use/could you use the reporting of adverse events in your sector? What is included and excluded from defining an adverse event? Does it matter? When sharing adverse events, what are the likely issues?

Public-sector Regulatory Bodies and Risk

> Organizations and society in general are thus facing new
> systemic risks that have arisen for the most part in the second
> half of the twenty-first century ... Among these new risks are
> major technological dangers (for example, Bhopal, Chernobyl,
> Three Mile Island, AZF-Toulouse), food-borne diseases (for
> example, mad cow disease, listeriosis), health threats (for
> example, the contaminated blood crisis, SARS, AIDS, H1N1)
> and environmental risks (for example, global warming,
> accumulation of pollutants, thinning of the ozone layer)
> (Lalonde and Boiral, 2012: p. 273).

Public-sector regulators have the responsibility of protecting the public
against a range of risks relevant to their sector. In this section, we look at
the tools and perspectives available to them.

The Precautionary Principle – Better Safe than Sorry

The European Union (EU), in dealing with uncertain risks, adopts the
Precautionary Principle (PP) as a legal principle. Complex, uncertain, and
ambiguous risks often lack conclusive scientific proof of cause and effect.
However, PP is a political and ethical response as well as a scientific one:

> When human activities may lead to morally unacceptable harm
> that is scientifically plausible but uncertain, actions shall be
> taken to avoid or diminish that harm.
> Morally unacceptable harm refers to harm to humans or the
> environment that is:
> * Threatening to human life or health, or
> * Serious and effectively irreversible, or
> * Inequitable to present or future generations, or
> * Imposed without adequate consideration of the human
>   rights of those affected (COMEST/UNESCO, 2005: p. 14).

The long delay in identifying deaths related to asbestosis is a justification
for the Precautionary Principle (COMEST/UNESCO, 2005). Alerts to the
dangers of asbestos and associated lung disease were first raised in 1898

but it was not until 1999 that the substance was banned in Europe:

> Health experts estimate that in the European Union (EU)
> alone, some 250,000 – 400,000 deaths from mesothelioma,
> lung cancer, and asbestosis will occur over the next 35 years,
> as a consequence of exposure to asbestos in the past
> (COMEST/UNESCO, 2005: p. 10).

The PP shifts the burden of proving tolerable risk to those who create risks. It encourages the analysis of alternatives and participatory decision-making methods.

However, the Precautionary Principle has its critics (Black, 2010c):

- It assumes that the application of the PP will result in a no-risk outcome. However, in the development of a medicine that could save lives, invoking PP may in fact lose lives

- PP works against 'trading off' risks. DDT, a once commonly used insecticide, has been banned in the US and Europe for some time but it is a chemical that is very effective against malaria. Controlled use of the DDT is now allowed in areas at risk from malaria (EPA, 2015)

- Finally, it can be used to protect national and commercial interests by denying the import of products that are deemed high risk.

Notwithstanding, the PP aligns well with a notion of public interest from a regulatory perspective. However, it can also be used to protect and reduce the number and extent of risks to which regulatory bodies are exposed thus constraining innovation and development.

Risk Prioritization and Strategic Evaluation

For a regulatory body, an important question is which risks to prioritise? Legislation and mandate identifies the risks it was set up to address but in any sector, there are new risks that require constant scanning. Which risks regulators choose is carefully scrutinized for effectiveness and value for money especially where there are a large number of regulatory personnel (Paoli and Wiles, 2015). Are the risks the right ones? Which risks can be reduced the most?

The choice of risks determines where resources will flow. Where little is known about a threat or hazard but it has severely negative consequences, there may be limited risk-reduction available. Precautionary approaches may also be appropriate. An alternative is to increase the resilience of the system by making decisions that are reversible (e.g. trial releases of a treatment or medicine), flexibility to increase the flow of resources to the risk or action on early warnings. Concentrating resources on a risk that is not resolvable may be unwise. On the other hand, the risk may suddenly explode.

Prioritisation is not a straightforward process. Risk-management strategies may be effective, efficient and sustainable but are they acceptable to stakeholders and are the ethics of the distribution of risk (who bears the most risk) fair?

Separating Public and Enterprise Risk-management

Safeguarding against Complex, Uncertain and Ambiguous risks raises for government regulators a number of dilemmas:

- The tendency to be over-cautious
- A reluctance to scan for new risks
- Risk-management to protect the organization rather than the public.

Which definition of risk should public sector organisations use? Recently, some public sector organizations have used the ERM definition of risk to construct risk-assessment and risk-management profiles:

---

risk is the effect of uncertainty on objectives (ISO, 2009).

For some, this definition is seen as inappropriate for public sector bodies, set up to protect the public good:

In the private sector, risk assessment focuses on the possible adverse effects of a risk on the organization itself, to business value as perceived by shareholders and financial markets; in the public sector "risk is more about systemic risks of failure to deliver services to citizens (Paoli and Wiles, 2015: p. 25).

This can lead to a risk-management approach that appears to put protection of the organisation on the same level as protection of the public.

A recently published risk matrix for staff and public consumption reveals that the impact category of 'adverse publicity' for the organization has the same impact rating and risk matrix score as 'death or permanent incapacity' to members of the public - an insensitive combination for a public body.

Risk-based Resource Allocation

Using the methods above, regulatory bodies devise risk-based regulation models (Black and Baldwin, 2010):

- Prioritising risks either through a risk governance approach by regulatory body choice
- Choosing what risks to tolerate - the regulator cannot control all risks. There are normally political considerations here
- Identifying the two general groups of risk
    - The risks that are intrinsic to a businesses' activities and
    - The effectiveness of a firm's management of its own risk
- Devising a scoring system to enable the regulator to compare firms against each other. This could result in the traffic light coding of red, orange and green or a simple high, medium and low.

The final stage is to link the risk-based regulation scheme to resource allocation, known as 'the principle of proportionality':

resources expended to control risk, (are) proportionate to the level of risk (Paoli and Wiles, 2015: p. 5).

Being able to compare an organisation's level of risk enables the regulatory body to strategically deploy staff to cover high and medium-risk enterprises and thus reduce the inspection or audit frequency on enterprises that present a low risk. The low-risk firm may get an extended frequency of visit, say once every four years.

Beneficiaries of Risk-targeting

Who benefits from risk-based regulation? Is it the regulatory body, the government, the business community or the public? Is it all these groups? Asking who benefits sharpens the use of the risk concept and reveals risk as contentious.

If the regulatory body sees its role as simply making sure that people are compliant with the rules, standards and regulations, then any instance of non-compliance becomes a risk for the regulator. Consequently, any breach of a law or rule, no matter how minor, such as not displaying a certificate of registration, may be defined as high risk - the risk attached to the rule infringed is irrelevant (Rothstein, 2003).

In contrast, the public understandably expects that the risks managed by regulators are those with the greatest potential for severe harm to the greatest number (Blanc, 2012: p. 72-73).

Judging who might be the beneficiaries of risk-based regulation is contentious because its introduction has coincided with the reduction of regulatory budgets. There have been conflicting arguments that risk-based regulation reduces risks overall (Environment Agency) but also claims that, due to resulting budget cuts, it actually *raises* the risks for the public (Tombs and Whyte, 2013).

Summary of Risk-based Regulation

There are six elements to risk-based regulation:

- It intends to control risk not by direct management but by auditing and overseeing the way that businesses and organisations *themselves* control risk

- It can be used as a device for allocating regulatory visits and audits

- It can be reactive by simply looking for hazards

- It can be further developed to require that the controls businesses use to manage their most frequent or critical risks conform to appropriate levels of residual risk

- The regulatory body and the individual regulator have a responsibility and a role in being proactive in disseminating information on critical risk, adverse events and quality processes.

- The central regulatory skills required for risk-based regulation are the effective inspection and audit of risk-management practices and the assessment and audit of risk and safety management systems (Gunningham, 2012).

> **Apply to your work**
>
> In relation to your own sector, what are the advantages of risk-based regulation and what are the disadvantages?

Things can change very quickly for regulated firms and agencies. Complacency, changes of management, downturns in the economy, poor suppliers; any of these may quickly turn a low risk beacon into a high risk incendiary. Therefore, the accuracy and sensitivity of the regulators' risk-assessment knowledge is fundamental to the meaningful management of risk in a sector.

Your regulatory body will have in place a risk-management approach suited to your sector. Having read this chapter you will better appreciate the issues involved and how to deal flexibly and creatively with the notion of risk. We now turn to the practice of regulating using the three-stage model: Plan, Inspect, Improve.

Chapter Four: Plan

Objectives

After reading this chapter, you will be able to:

- Create a risk-assessment
- Analyse relevant issues and risks
- Set your inspection/audit questions using Pyramid Planning
- Produce an evidence collection plan
- Act in the event of contact from a whistleblower
- Make practical arrangements for such an event
- Consider providing guidance to the regulated organisation
- Avoid common problems such as ritual compliance.

Rationale

The purpose of planning the inspection or audit is to ensure that:

- The results are meaningful to stakeholders
- The conclusions address significant and appropriate regulatory issues
- Sufficient, relevant and reliable evidence support the conclusions.

Drawing on analysis of the issues and the relevant standards, regulations and risk-assessment, the inspection/audit plan identifies the main question(s), evidence criteria and evidence-collection methods. The plan anticipates problems, such as the possibility of regulatory capture and ritual compliance. Planning is not an activity restricted to this stage but may continue throughout.

What Type of Inspection/audit is it?

Your organisation will probably use different types of inspection or audit that may vary in intensity, frequency, focus, number of members, content or time allocated. It may be a follow-up or a licensing audit, or response to a complaint and it may be announced or unannounced. Many regulatory bodies also require audits of health and safety systems and/or quality management systems.

Announced/unannounced

For an announced inspection, the regulator or auditor will inform the organisation, with suitable notice, of the inspection date and the people and documents that should be available. This may include consumers and advocates.

An unannounced inspection comes with no forewarning of any kind – the inspector arrives at the door bearing identification and requests entry.

Using both a systematic review and a research study on the practice of making announced versus unannounced inspections, Klerks et al concluded:

> Dutch nursing homes were inspected, unannounced, and later announced, in order to compare the risks detected during the inspections. It is concluded that unannounced inspections did not reveal more or different risks, but provided a better insight into the quality of care delivered. Announced inspections are the best option for the assessment both of the organisation and of its preconditions for good care (Klerks et al., 2013).

The frequency of announced as against unannounced inspections varies across sectors and countries although, as an aid to inspiring public confidence in the regulatory system, the unannounced is gaining credibility.

Planning for an Inspection

The stages in planning the inspection/audit are shown in Figure 17. A first step is to become familiar with the production processes, services and environments that will be inspected. Many regulatory staff are professionals drawn from the specific sector, but there is still a need to keep abreast of trends in risk and policy, update best practice and become familiar with the individual circumstances of a location or enterprise.

Analysis starts with a risk-assessment, which takes in the current issues. Inspection/audit questions identify specific issues and an evidence-collection plan is produced. Finally, there are practical arrangements to be made.

Figure 17: Planning Your Work

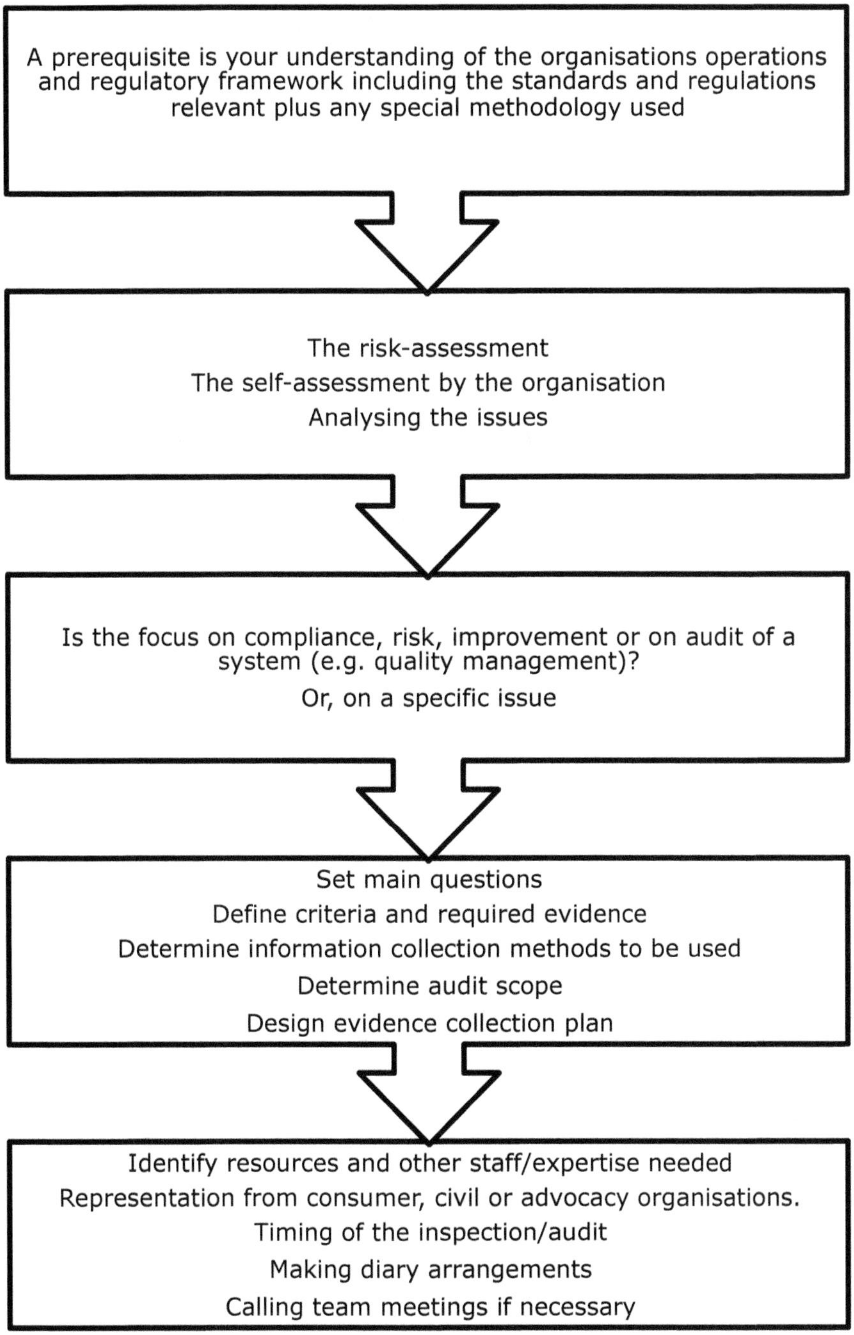

A prerequisite is your understanding of the organisations operations and regulatory framework including the standards and regulations relevant plus any special methodology used

The risk-assessment

The self-assessment by the organisation

Analysing the issues

Is the focus on compliance, risk, improvement or on audit of a system (e.g. quality management)?

Or, on a specific issue

Set main questions

Define criteria and required evidence

Determine information collection methods to be used

Determine audit scope

Design evidence collection plan

Identify resources and other staff/expertise needed

Representation from consumer, civil or advocacy organisations.

Timing of the inspection/audit

Making diary arrangements

Calling team meetings if necessary

Your Planning Addresses Current and Past Issues

There may be a range of current issues for which to plan:

- Complaints received about the organisation
- Self-assessment of compliance supplied by the organisation, if required
- Issues that arose in a previous inspection/audit which are still outstanding (check any action plans and follow-up)
- Original and current risk-assessments
- Any hazards or adverse events reported from the organisation or from organisations in the sector that might be relevant
- Current interventions and checks the regulator is running, for example, a Food Safety Rating Scheme
- Feedback from consumers, interested others and end-users; a small random sample is used to survey users of a service, for example a school
- Liaison with other regulatory bodies
- Contact with police or other authorities concerning the organisation
- Issues raised by the media concerning an organisation
- Contact through whistleblowing
- Professional and sector issues arising that may influence the standards being used
- Internal audit information on health, safety and quality management systems.

> Apply to your work
>
> In the context of your own work, are there further issues you could add?

Analysing the Issues

Significant issues may include risk, compliance, management systems and performance.

Regulatory bodies are concerned with whether the management of an organisation is controlling risks inherent to their sector. This could relate to data protection, school achievement, workplace safety, child protection or food-borne illness. This concern is not limited to that moment in time but also whether management controls of safety, quality and risk are sustainable in the future.

There are a number of basic questions to consider:

- Are standards, regulations or rules being met?
- What are the inherent risks and residual risks?
- Are management systems performing well now and are they likely to perform in the future?
- Where does accountability lie?
- What are the outcomes for end-users?
- What are the issues of rights, values, principles, citizenship and participation?
- Are issues of economy, efficiency and effectiveness relevant?

Having considered these questions, the first planning task is to create a risk-assessment.

Undertaking a Risk-assessment

Risk-based regulation is:

> Concerned with the anticipation of what could happen, aiming
> to reduce actual harm by anticipation and prevention. It is
> explicitly designed in terms of systematic risk assessment and
> prioritization (Hutter and Lloyd-Bostock, 2013: p. 3).

The risk-assessment is an important step in selecting the main questions
for the inspection/audit. Risk matrix scoring produced by your own
regulatory body may support the assessment and/or probability based
calculations using research. Chapter Three revealed that risk is often about
uncertainties. Your intuitions on their own may not be sufficient but they
derive from your sector expertise and should be taken into account.

Below is a simple outline of the process.

Figure 18: The Risk Assessment Process

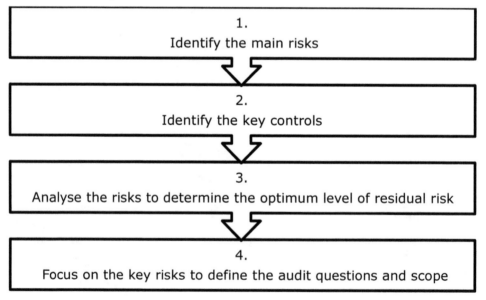

Below are the steps of the risk-assessment.

Step 1

Every industry and enterprise engages with risks that may produce harm. You probably know what the high, medium and low inherent risks of your sector are. Nevertheless, a risk-assessment cannot be general as it focuses directly on the organisation being inspected/audited.

Chapter Two suggested that asking the following questions could help to identify inherent risk:

- Which processes generate most concern?
- Which processes generate the most errors or present the most risk to safety?
- Which processes appear unpredictable or unmanaged?
- Which processes contain bottlenecks
- Which processes contain unexpected minor errors that may combine into a serious risk?

Chapter 2 also described the difference between inherent risk and residual risk and explained the function of controls. The diagram below illustrates the meaning of residual risk.

Figure 19: The Calculation of Residual Risk

Risks are relevant, dependent on the remit of a particular regulator. For example, personal data will be the main focus of a data protection regulator, while the quality of external audit is relevant to a public company accounts oversight body and so on.

Step 2

The next step is to match each inherent risk to the key control or controls that should be in place. At this stage, you should identify if possible the key management and control processes, including Information Technology (IT) systems. Equally important is how the control mechanisms are monitored, who controls the monitoring and what is done with the results.

Step 3

For each control, you need to make a professional judgement, or seek further expertise, on what the optimum level of residual-risk should be, i.e. the level of risk considered tolerable. Later in the inspection/audit, you will want to know if controls are in place and whether those controls secure the optimum level of residual risk.

Step 4

Finally, from inherent risks, controls and resulting residual risks, the ones that are the most relevant to this inspection or audit should be selected. It is likely that this risk-assessment will be the basis for your main inspection question but you may need to include current and past issues and other case-specific priorities.

> Apply to your work
>
> How do you determine the level of residual risk in your sector? Can it be reduced to zero risk?

It is sometimes the case that regulators combine measurable standards and regulations alongside broader principle-based standards. Nevertheless, each type of standard will require supporting evidence. The section below on the inspection/audit plan is a means of creating main questions for that specific organisation taking into account its individual circumstances and linking them with standards and regulations.

Pyramid Planning

This section explains how to create an inspection/audit plan using pyramid planning (Minto, 1987).

With any inspection or audit, there is always a main question. It may be general, such as –

> **'Is the organisation compliant with all the standards?'**

Or specific, such as –

> **'Are management safety controls working effectively?'**

There may be a series of main questions required for each inspection/audit by the regulatory body.

These questions will have a 'yes' or 'no' answer because at the end of the inspection or audit, an auditor should be able to say, 'Yes, the controls are working effectively', or 'No, they are not working effectively'.

The main question requires clear evidence to derive an answer because your inspection/audit is evidence-based. However, it is a broad question. In order to determine the specific evidence required you break the question down into its constituent parts.

Your analysis of the risk assessment and issues informs your main question and from this (Level 1) you:

- Create sub-questions (Level 2)
- Identify the evidence criteria to answer each question (Level 3)
- Plan collection of evidence (Level 4)

- Plan Information-collection Methods and Analysis (Level 5).

Figure 20: Pyramid Planning

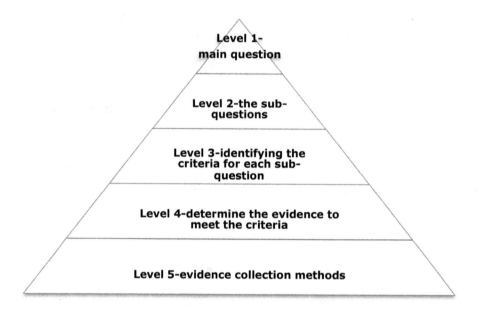

Each of these levels forms the pyramid. You can have more levels - it depends on how complex the main question is - but the pyramid should contain the five levels above. There can be more than one main question.

Let us look at an example in more detail by breaking the main question down into a number of levels each of which contains sub-questions. Analysis of the main question identifies the evidence needed for the answer (the criteria) and the method you will use to meet those criteria.

Level 1 Main question	Is the organisation compliant with the relevant standards?

This is an all-encompassing question and we need to break it down into the specific standards (we will use two for the example). We will clarify at **Level 2** the meaning of 'relevant standards'.

Level 2	Standard 1: Does the organisation have a valid complaints system?
Breaking down the main question	
	Standard 2: Does the organisation offer counselling to customers?

Level 2 clarifies the relevant standards, describing them and any conditions attached to them. You can see that level 2 reveals further questions such as:

- Is the complaints system valid?
- Is counselling available to customers?

We therefore need to find if the firm meets the conditions for successful achievement of the standards. We need to know this in order to make the decision on whether or not the organisation is compliant. The next level will provide the criteria to answer these questions:

Level 3	
Establish the criteria	Does the complaints system conform to best practice?
	Are complaints dealt with on time?
	Are qualified counselling personnel employed?
	Is there more than 75% satisfaction with the service?

At Level 3 we have reached the point where we can answer the questions because we have identified the criteria necessary:

- Level 4 clarifies the evidence needed to satisfy the criteria
- Level 5 identifies the methods used to collect the evidence.

Levels 4 and 5 are shown in the diagram below.

Figure 21: Pyramid Planning Example

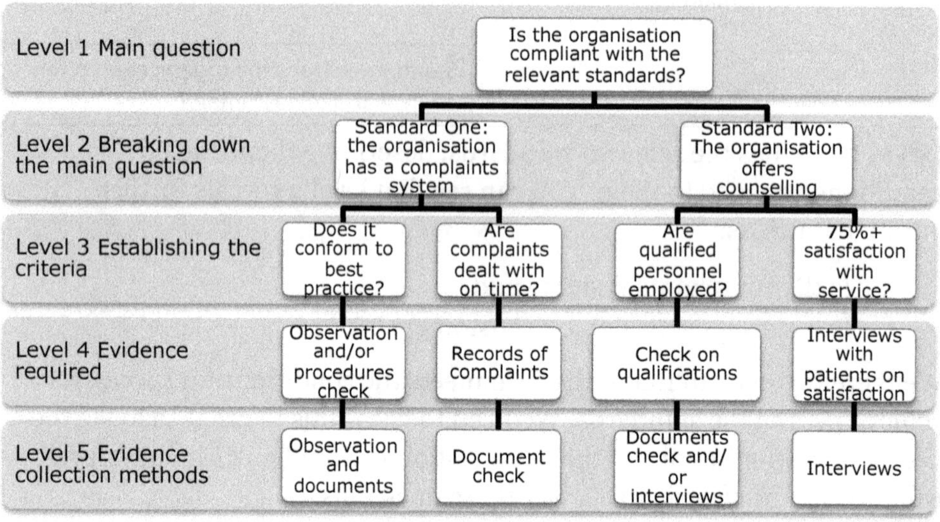

Level 1 Main question			Is the organisation compliant with the relevant standards?		
Level 2 Breaking down the main question		Standard One: the organisation has a complaints system		Standard Two: The organisation offers counselling	
Level 3 Establishing the criteria	Does it conform to best practice?	Are complaints dealt with on time?	Are qualified personnel employed?	75%+ satisfaction with service?
Level 4 Evidence required	Observation and/or procedures check	Records of complaints	Check on qualifications	Interviews with patients on satisfaction
Level 5 Evidence collection methods	Observation and documents	Document check	Documents check and/ or interviews	Interviews

The questions and criteria form a hierarchy with evidence-collection methods at the base.

You now have a plan where your main question links to the evidence and the collection methods. At the end of an inspection/audit, it will be possible to determine if the organisation is compliant with all the standards. Of course, your answer will be more detailed, for example, 'Yes, but'.... this provides a discussion point around strengths and weaknesses.

The benefits of this method include the following:

- The inspection is available and transparent to all

- It shows objectivity and fairness

- It enables you to check that you have included all the relevant factors

- When working with many, possibly complex, standards and a team of auditors or inspectors, it offers a means of dividing the work where each party understands their contribution

- It offers a structure for use at the feedback stage to draw together conclusions, new insights, new risks and the quality of the evidence

- Collection methods are identified (surveys, questionnaires, interview schedules), which can be standardised across a team or locations

- It does not exclude allowing the plan to change and evidence from other sources to be collected. It should not be an investigative straitjacket.

Some regulators may hold the view that if the rules are complied with, there is no need to investigate further. However, other regulators may have the *improvement* of the enterprise as an objective.

> Apply to your work
>
> Compile a pyramid plan using your last inspection/audit. Is there a main question or more than one? Complete all the levels to understand how they link the questions to the criteria, to the evidence and finally to the methods.

Quality Management Systems and Pyramid Planning

The example below has the main question:

'Are compliance controls at XYZ firm effective?

The analysis explores the nature and extent of compliance over a time-period as one thread of the pyramid. A further thread analyses the compliance controls in place and another assesses management controls over the compliance unit. Often a regulator requires compliance with a particular quality management scheme or set of private standards.

The aim of Pyramid Planning is to create a logical, transparent plan, to consider what can be done in the time available, and if a smaller body of evidence should be used.

An auditor/inspector may combine any number of main questions.

Figure 22: Auditing Compliance Controls

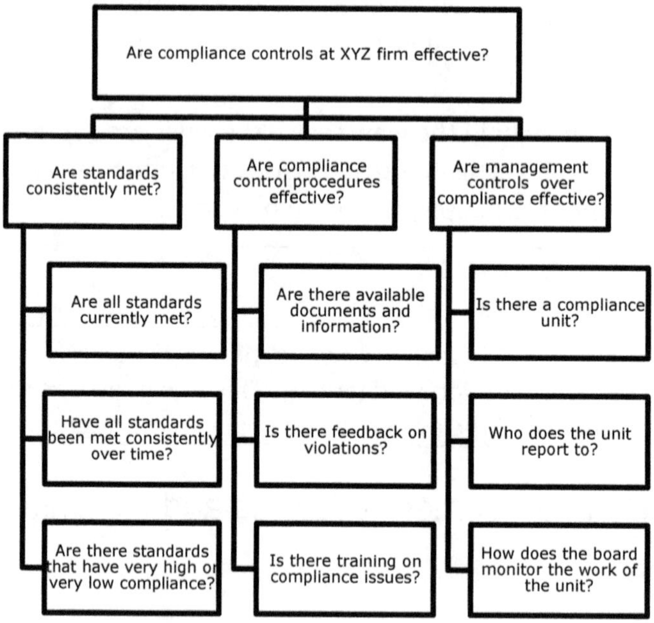

```
                    ┌─────────────────────────────────────────┐
                    │ Are compliance controls at XYZ firm       │
                    │ effective?                                │
                    └─────────────────────────────────────────┘
        ┌──────────────────────┼──────────────────────┐
┌───────────────┐    ┌──────────────────┐    ┌──────────────────┐
│ Are standards │    │ Are compliance   │    │ Are management   │
│ consistently  │    │ control          │    │ controls over    │
│ met?          │    │ procedures       │    │ compliance       │
│               │    │ effective?       │    │ effective?       │
└───────────────┘    └──────────────────┘    └──────────────────┘
┌───────────────┐    ┌──────────────────┐    ┌──────────────────┐
│ Are all       │    │ Are there        │    │ Is there a       │
│ standards     │    │ available        │    │ compliance unit? │
│ currently     │    │ documents and    │    │                  │
│ met?          │    │ information?     │    │                  │
└───────────────┘    └──────────────────┘    └──────────────────┘
┌───────────────┐    ┌──────────────────┐    ┌──────────────────┐
│ Have all      │    │ Is there         │    │ Who does the     │
│ standards     │    │ feedback on      │    │ unit report to?  │
│ been met      │    │ violations?      │    │                  │
│ consistently  │    │                  │    │                  │
│ over time?    │    │                  │    │                  │
└───────────────┘    └──────────────────┘    └──────────────────┘
┌───────────────┐    ┌──────────────────┐    ┌──────────────────┐
│ Are there     │    │ Is there         │    │ How does the     │
│ standards     │    │ training on      │    │ board monitor    │
│ that have     │    │ compliance       │    │ the work of the  │
│ very high or  │    │ issues?          │    │ unit?            │
│ very low      │    │                  │    │                  │
│ compliance?   │    │                  │    │                  │
└───────────────┘    └──────────────────┘    └──────────────────┘
```

The Inspection/audit Scope

Select the sub-questions to fit the scope of the inspection/audit:

- Is the scope the total activities of an organisation or only one part, such as health and safety?
- Is the organisation located in one place or are there multiple sites?
- Are site visits necessary and if so how many?
- Will the plan fit within your time constraints?
- Who are the management personnel accountable for the control of the area of the inspection/audit?

Sources of Inspection/audit Criteria

Where standards are the basis for questions, the criteria and evidence needed are normally specified within the standard.

However, the use of criteria from standards is rarely straightforward. They are open to *interpretation,* particularly in the case of flexible standards. For example, criteria for process standards are very specific while principle-based standards are broad. Even if the criteria for standards are specific, to what level must the criteria be achieved for compliance? Is X enough or not quite enough? Often guidance for regulatory staff is vague (Walshe and Phipps, 2013). This point is particularly relevant in relation to flexible standards where discussion with colleagues and managers on interpretation and professional principles/values will be important.

There will be circumstances where it is necessary to consider other sources of evidence criteria.

Table 4: Sources of Inspection/audit Criteria (adapted from ECA, 2013b)

Criteria based on legislation, regulations and standards are generally accepted. So too are private standards as with ISO or API
Generally accepted are sources such as professional associations, academic literature and expert opinion or good practice
There may be instances where none of the above is available. Benchmarking (comparing with another organisation), consultation or developing standards through the inspector/auditors' own analysis may be the only option. The latter would require agreement through the team and/or by those inspected.

What is Evidence?

The following approaches to the notion of evidence are relevant for inspection and audit:

- Evidence can be defined as that which tends to prove the existence or non-existence of a fact (Blackburn, 2008)
- It is important to use an evidence-collection process that is methodical and which minimises bias and allows for the consideration of contradictory evidence to disprove the favoured point of view. Evidentiary cherry-picking should be avoided
- Evidence should be considered inadmissible if it is poorly presented, incorrectly labelled or not completely accurate – for example, if a photo or video is of poor quality.

The evidence gathered serves multiple purposes, including the following:

- Proving that standards are achieved or not
- Proving that criminal violations have or have not taken place
- Providing a basis for grading or star ratings.

Evidence can include:

- Physical evidence such as objects found at or absent from the location
- Statements or testimonials from witnesses
- Maps, diagrams, sketches, videos, photographs and any other indicative evidence. Significant documents, such as records of staffing or care, injury logs, transactions, cleaning and waste schedules and policies and procedures
- Expert opinion and professional judgement.

The evidence should be sufficient and appropriate.

The quantity of evidence is sufficient if, when taken as a whole, it is adequate to provide persuasive support for the contents of the (inspection/audit) report. For evidence to be appropriate, the information must be relevant, reliable and valid. In exercising professional judgment, auditors and inspectors should ask themselves if the collective weight of evidence is enough to persuade a reasonable person that observations and conclusions are valid and that the recommendations are appropriate (Office of the Auditor General Canada, 2013).

Internally Commissioned Audits

Audits occur within organisations on a regular basis, in many cases using internal staff. Regulators may consider such audits a source of evidence yet be concerned as to their reliability.

When using either internal or external audits, the degree of independence involved provides a measure of reliability:

- First party audits refer to an organisation auditing itself and are also known as internal audits. These can have degrees of independence such as internal auditors from one branch, office or country auditing another branch of the same firm
- Second party audits describe when a company is audited by a supplier or partner
- Third party audits are the most independent and are most effectively achieved when executed by a relevant regulator. External independent auditors also perform these but the degree of independence is questioned as external auditors supply the service for a fee and may wish to supply other services and solicit repeat business (Fiolleau et al., 2013).

There is clearly common ground between external audits, internal audits and third part regulatory visits. Information available from these sources should be carefully assessed - the more independent the better (see Gadziala, 2005).

Apply to your work
What types of inspection/audit do you use? In what ways could you demonstrate the independence of your judgements?

Determine Information-collection Methods

Chapter Five discusses a range of information-collection methods. A principle is that regulators gather primary evidence and regulated organisations provide secondary evidence. Evidence obtained through the team's direct physical examination, observation, calculation and inspection is generally more reliable than evidence obtained indirectly from secondary sources (Office of the Auditor General Canada, 2013).

Given that there may be doubt over the accuracy and quality of documents obtained from those inspected or audited, it is necessary to *confirm* that accuracy and quality. Triangulation is one method of checking the validity of information from various standpoints (this is developed in Chapter 5).

Evidence-collection Uses Triangulation

An evidence-collection plan will use secondary evidence by subjecting it to testing through triangulation (see figure below).

Figure 23: Showing Triangulation of Evidence Sources

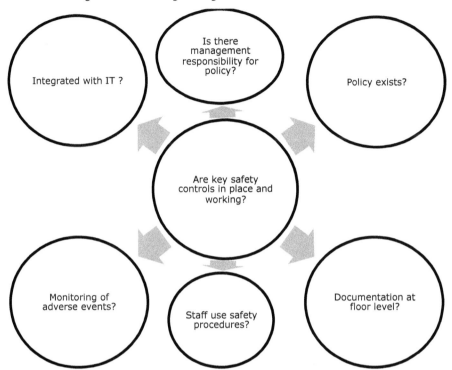

Figure 23 is an example of triangulation:

- Interviews with staff confirm if floor-level documentation is read
- Minutes of meetings confirm if management are actively responsible for policy
- There should be a policy on the monitoring of adverse events and that policy should be recognised as best practice.

Data Analysis Methods

Data analysis is the breaking down of large sets of data so that they can be easily understood. Often, presentation of data is key and there are three approaches recognized by social science research:

- Qualitative analysis (the findings will not be generalisable to wider populations)
- Quantitative analysis (based on probability theory and sampling) – the findings are generalisable to a wider population
- A combination of both.

For most inspections and audits, there is a dependence on qualitative analysis but quantitative surveys of wider populations such as school children or shareholders also occur. The time available for such surveys in regulation is limited but it may be deemed necessary.

Think about the People You Will Work With

An inspection team may consist of professionals from an appropriate industry and/or users of the organisation's product or service, e.g. in the inspection of medical training.

Lay Assessors

Some regulatory bodies use lay assessors whose function is to represent the public's point of view. These lay assessors are drawn from the public and may be part of an end-user group. They assist regulation staff in evaluating the quality of service and typically do not require any qualifications beyond a genuine interest in the organisation, product or service under audit. Any necessary training, support and expenses are given. Lay assessors typically contact and survey the end-user more frequently than regulators and in a more informal setting, the aim of which is to become a trusted intermediary (Simmill-Binning et al., 2007). It is best practice to use a buddy system where an experienced lay assessor accompanies a new lay assessor to help that person acclimatise. The senior auditor will have a strategy on the deployment of lay assessors.

> Apply to your work
>
> Lay assessors play an important part in increasing the consumer and citizen voice in regulation. What role do they have in the inspection/audit? How do they contribute to the final report?

Practical Arrangements

Planning is necessary to allocate tasks and coordinate diaries, travel and accommodation. For an announced inspection or audit, the regulatory authority will contact the organisation to make arrangements. Regulated organisations put considerable effort into preparing for an inspection (see Walshe et al., 2014: p. 15) and, in preparation, may contact other organisations such as a volunteer oversight group or the representative of a local authority.

Whistleblowing and Inspection

Employees revealing illegality, immorality, cruelty and abuse within their organisations have been responsible for bringing to justice and exposing the perpetrators of significant criminality and brutality. 18.3% of corporate fraud cases in large US companies between 1996 and 2004 were detected and brought forward by employees (Kaptein, 2011). In the UK, the abuse of people in care at Winterbourne View care home (Flynn, 2012) and hospital care tragedies at Mid-Staffordshire General Hospital (Kennedy, 2001, Francis, 2010) together with revelations on press intrusion (Leveson, 2012) highlighted the role of the whistleblower in exposing wrongdoing.

Whistleblowers are defined as persons who attempt to stop or change wrongdoing inside their own organisations:

- By using an internal whistleblowing procedure
- By going externally to an authority that has the power to stop the wrongdoing (Near and Miceli, 1985)
- By approaching the press who have the power to name and shame.

Whistleblowers in most countries have some protected status from reprisal or dismissal. However, protection varies widely from one country to another and is significantly less certain for public and private sector subcontractors and consultants. (See Wolfe et al., 2014, Etienne, 2014). Often, there are prescribed regulators to whom whistleblowers must take their complaint. Whistleblowing is not the same as a complaint from a member of the public or an exposé by a pressure group, as with the recent campaign by People for the Ethical Treatment of Animals (2014) drawing attention to cruelty and abuse in Australian sheep shearing stations.

Whistleblowers offer a unique insight into the organisation with which they are connected but very often regulators do not respond positively - in fact, there are more reports of them ignoring whistleblowers than acting on their information (James, 2011, Annakin, 2011). Most whistleblowers have first raised their complaint through an internal process; many will only raise it twice before stopping (Vandekerckhove et al., 2013). If ignored, most whistleblowers will give up. In fact, only 50% of those who want to change wrongdoing in their workplace actually complain. Most are deterred, not by the threat of reprisal, but by a culture of 'deafness' (Jones and Kelly, 2014) - they are simply ignored. Where there is reprisal, it is not in the form of instant dismissal but as 'a series of actions designed to isolate, humiliate or harass whistleblowers without leaving a trail of evidence' (Annakin, 2011: p. 281).

The following points may help:

- When contacted by a whistleblower, an authority should always investigate
- Make sure you are up to date with the region's whistleblowing legislation (in some countries, there is state-to-state variation)
- Make sure that workers in the organisation have the authority's contact information and feel confident they know they are contacting the prescribed organisation for whistleblowing complaints in that sector. If the whistleblower goes to the wrong regulator, they may not have protected status
- Make yourself available to staff as you walk around
- Find out if there is a specialised agency for whistleblower reprisal and protection (in Canada there is)
- It should be remembered that protected status may also give anonymity
- If required, the whistleblower should be met outside the place of work.

Legislation gives protection against reprisal. In some countries, this is defined widely to include social reprisals, lack of training, dead-end tasks. However, the outcome for the whistleblower is consistently poor, particularly in relation to obtaining future employment.

Notification by a whistleblower should trigger alarm; it implies that the management and culture is unable to manage change and risk in work practices. Be aware of good practice in internal procedures for whistleblowing (Public Concern at Work, 2013, Roberts et al., 2011, Miceli et al., 2009).

Improving Whistleblowing Practice

Recommendations to regulators to improve whistleblowing practice include the following:

- Encourage, urge or require – with threat of withholding licence if necessary – organisations to have internal whistleblowing procedures
- Regulators should have their own clear procedures for responding to whistleblowers who approach them
- Have an annual reporting mechanism of whistleblower contacts and outcomes (Public Concern at Work, 2013).

> Apply to your work
>
> Using the Internet, briefly research the role of whistleblowers in exposing wrongdoing in your sector. How do you plan your work to be prepared for contact from a whistleblower?

Be Ready to Use Your Regulatory Powers

Look again at the powers you have through the legal framework (see Chapter 1) or through sanctions and persuasion.

- Do you need to take any special equipment with you?
- Are you confident about powers of entry?
- Do you have the appropriate ID? It would be legitimate for an organisation to refuse you entry if you did not have a valid ID.

It is useful to know the various levers that assist you in the regulatory task. The following should also be kept in mind:

- There may be an audit committee or health and safety staff within the firm
- It may be possible to deploy recent complaints or comments from consumers
- There may be international and national standards that overlap with your own standards
- Civil standards and their organisations may also provide leverage.

Even if you are only used to thinking about sanctions and your own legal powers, these other regulatory levers are powerful and should be built into your planning.

Target Beneficiaries of the Inspection

It is best to consider who will be the eventual beneficiaries of an inspection and who else may be influenced. It is advantageous to remember what the standards or regulations are designed to achieve, what problems they are meant to overcome. Safety and protection might be high on the agenda but so too should be quality, improvement and fair dealing. This will give the scope of the inspection. Obviously, management and staff of the organisation will be an objective for feedback, as will end-users. It also may be worth considering, at the planning stage, how and where to feedback the results of the inspection to stakeholders.

The inspection/audit is of benefit to the public in improving goods and services and preventing abuse and exploitation. It is also of benefit to contract commissioners, suppliers and those who will purchase goods to use in their own production process. It gives an independent external viewpoint on the performance of the organisation and an assurance of sound corporate conduct and quality.

> Apply to your work
>
> Focusing on your last inspection, who were the beneficiaries?

Guidance

As part of the planning process, it might be worth considering any guidance, either verbally or with specific written materials, which should be communicated. Regulators routinely provide guidance and the UK Hampton Report (Hampton, 2005) and European sources have recommended greater provision of guidance and greater clarity with regard to the legislation and regulations:

Government guidance is currently produced and disseminated in a way that leaves Small Medium Enterprises (SMEs) with a great deal of uncertainty, both deterring them from using it and creating additional costs for their businesses. Many businesses are also unclear about whether following guidance means they have complied with the law. They do not always know where to get the right help (Anderson, 2008: p. 6).

Research suggests that small businesses are not equipped to deal with complex inspection requirements (Fairman and Yapp, 2005, OECD, 2005).

Guidance helps both parties by having a point at which understanding can be checked – those regulated should not be doubtful about what is required of them.

Registration or Licensing

If involved in the licensing and registration event of the organisation concerned, the site visit is an ideal point to make sure the applicant has the appropriate understanding, not only of the standards but also what they can expect in a regulation visit and how they might prepare. For the applicant, the initial inspection may be the first time they have given serious thought to the rules and standards (Yapp and Fairman, 2006).

If not involved, be aware of the licensing process content, as this will help anticipate what the organisation ought to know and where any gaps might be.

Guidance will not impart the motivation to comply if that is missing, but taking the opportunity to talk with those audited or inspected gives a better understanding of motivation and disposition.

Anticipating the Risks of the Inspection/audit

This section identifies high-risk points that may delay the audit/inspection or put the quality of it at risk. It is better to prepare for potential problems at the planning stage than deal with those problems on site.

Ashworth et al. found that a sample of inspectors recognised five frequent risks or problems (2002). They are shown below together with how inspectors ranked them in regards to frequency and importance. We will go through each one in turn.

Table 5: Five Frequent Regulator Problems

Ranking	Problem
1	Regulatory capture
1	Performance ambiguity
2	Ritualistic compliance
2	Data problems
3	Resistance by regulatees
(Ashworth et al., 2002)	

Regulatory Capture

'Regulatory capture' occurs:

> when bureaucrats, regulators and politicians cease to serve some notion of a wider collective public interest and begin to systematically favour specific vested interests, usually the very interests they were supposed to regulate and restrain for the wider public interest (Baker, 2010: p. 648).

This broad definition emphasises that 'capture' occurs at political and regulator levels as well as at the individual regulator level. Examples of politically motivated capture occurred in the US Reagan administration - heads of regulatory bodies were appointed, already hostile to the idea of regulation itself. One such appointee, Anne McGill Burford, resigned as Administrator of the Environmental Protection Agency amid charges of political manipulation and mismanagement of a program to clean up toxic wastes (Wood and Waterman, 1991).

Capture at the level of regulatory staff may occur when:

- The inspector/auditor takes, on trust, information given or promises made
- The inspector/auditor identifies with the profession or business possibly by having come from that industry or wanting to return to that industry (Makkai and Braithwaite, 1992)
- Sympathy with the problems clouds impartial judgement
- The authority allows the organisation under inspection to set the agenda as to what is examined or lets the organisation get used to where and when the investigation takes place
- There is corruption or other misconduct by the inspector or organisation under inspection.

You can combat capture by:

- Instead of trusting the information provided, using evidence-based inspection, triangulation and checking (chapters 4,5)
- Controlling the relationship - using the principles of natural justice and procedural justice (Chapter 5) rather than valuations of character
- Being clear about the role of the inspector and the duties and responsibilities of the managers of the organisation. Avoiding 'fuzzy' boundaries
- Having the principles of your legislation or framework clearly in mind and referencing your decisions to what is in the public interest (Introduction)
- Being aware of rewards and inducements that may be extended
- Occasionally working in a team (Muehlenbachs et al., 2013) to look at the situation from a different perspective
- Changing routines or inspected organisations (Jin and Lee, 2012).

Performance Ambiguity

Performance ambiguity occurs where there is no agreement or clarity on the meaning of terms such as safety, welfare or quality. Mascini and Wijk point out that this problem is compounded when regulators themselves are inconsistent on definitions (2009). Ambiguity can be countered by:

- Being confident in the organisation's interpretation of the standard or term
- Providing guidance on definitions of terminology, using the inspection/audit plan
- Tailoring input to the abilities and experience of those inspected and/or audited
- Give all involved a chance to feedback and respond to findings (chapter 6).

Ritualistic Compliance

'Ritualistic compliance' (Power, 1994) occurs when an organisation simply goes through the motions of being regulated - it is a form of resistance. The organisation may have no serious intention of doing anything or taking any notice of the results of the inspection/audit. The regulator can engage with this problem by:

- Carrying out follow-up and repeat inspections
- Using responsive enforcement where there is the ability to comply but not the willingness (Chapter 6)
- Influencing the organisation using third-party organisations such as consumers, standards bodies or civil groups (Chapter 6).

Creative Compliance

Here the law is used to frustrate regulatory monitoring. It is a tactic of avoidance used by those with the money and the expertise to resist controls *legally*. In the UK, for example, when Tony Blair's government issued a directive to reduce National Health Service hospital waiting lists to 18 months, some Health Trusts approached the task to the letter of the directive rather than the spirit. They hurried to treat minor cases that had been waiting for nearly 18 months whilst cancelling the appointments of more urgent cases that had been on the waiting list a shorter time (Hood, 2006).

This is an example of Creative Compliance, which involves finding ways to accomplish compliance within the letter of the law whilst totally undermining the intended outcome.

This problem can be overcome by asking for cooperation and, if not forthcoming, by taking the details of your suspicions to your management team. In some cases a legal challenge is required.

Resistance

Some companies and institutions resist the imposition of regulation at all levels. They may do this for ideological reasons or because compliance is expensive or time-consuming. In the case of genuine deep-seated resistance, it is necessary to:

- Tackle each violation on its severity
- Use a responsive enforcement strategy to take into account the lack of willingness of those inspected (Chapter 6)
- Remind managers of their responsibilities and potential enforcement actions
- Check that there is not an underlying lack of ability to meet the standards or regulations viz. lack of understanding or lack of financial resources.

Sometimes the standards themselves may be trivial or wrongly applied and the resistance is understandable. For example, foster homes for people with disability are required to undergo the same regulatory regime as a large nursing home, which some would consider inappropriate. The inspector should inform management personnel of inappropriate application and draw on the experience of colleagues.

Data Problems

An inspector may find with small businesses that there is a problem with the collection of data – that there are no accounts and no safety records. Alternatively, it may be that a new organisation creates channels for gathering compliance material that may not conform to what is required.

Where the right quality of data is not forthcoming, it may be necessary to rely on inadequate or incomplete data or to trust data provided by the organisation, exposing the regulator to regulatory capture. Ways of dealing with this include:

- Remind those being inspected of any standards or legislation requiring management competency
- If appropriate, remind those regulated that it is an offence to withhold data
- See if you can gain leverage using data from the organisation's quality management system or from internal/external audit reports
- Cross check data supplied with other informants or intelligence gathered by your regulator.

Apply to your work

How did you tackle any or all of these problems and how might you improve your response in the future?

Other possible risks to your plan could arise from having prepared for more work than your team are able to complete. The inspection/audit plan should include a strategy for engaging with a particular problem should it be likely to occur.

Adapting to Your Context

In many inspection/audits, there is a common pattern to question setting and evidence-collection. It is advisable that the auditor/inspector become familiar with this and know where it is possible to take shortcuts. However, the method of selecting the plan for evidence-collection offered in this chapter gives a transparent, open and communicable strategy, linking the required evidence with the preferred collection method.

Planning gives structure but it also advisable to be both open to new risks that emerge and flexible in response to evidence that contradicts assumptions.

A Checklist for Planning

- Identify type of inspection/audit
- Gather information on current and past issues including questionnaires, data supplied and communications
- Create a risk-assessment
- Identify the main issues
- What are the standards or criteria used?
- Create a plan for your inspection/audit using Pyramid Planning
- Identify the beneficiaries of the inspection
- Establish if there has been contact with whistleblowers
- Establish who is involved in the inspection. Do they have the necessary information and details? Is the organization prepared (announced inspection only)?
- Determine guidance specific to this organisation
- Update any area of professional expertise required
- Remind yourself of the powers of inspection/audit
- Plan a response to any possible problems in planning as outlined in this chapter.

We now turn to the Inspect stage of the PII model.

Chapter Five: Inspect

Objectives

After reading this chapter you will be able to:

- Implement the inspection/audit plan
- Understand the importance of the first meeting
- Adopt a balanced and fair approach to your work
- Use evidence-based inspection
- Select appropriate information-collection methods and know their strengths and weaknesses
- Implement 'triangulation' for gathering and confirming evidence
- Correctly use a contemporaneous notebook and be able to take a witness statement
- Check your information/evidence-collection for bias, accuracy and completeness.

Rationale

The purpose of this stage is to meet the organisation being regulated, recognise individual circumstances and collect data to achieve the evidence-collection plan.

The ability to use a variety of information-collection methods is essential. Methodical collection of data enhances its value as evidence in feedback or in court. A common failing is that collection methods are unmethodical, biased or incomplete and are, as a result, limited in their effectiveness.

This stage explains the concepts of triangulation, drilling down, case-tracking and audit trails. It also looks at the interpretation of data and analysis.

The Inspection/Audit Process

Figure 24: The Inspection/audit Process (INTOSAI, 2004: p. 63)

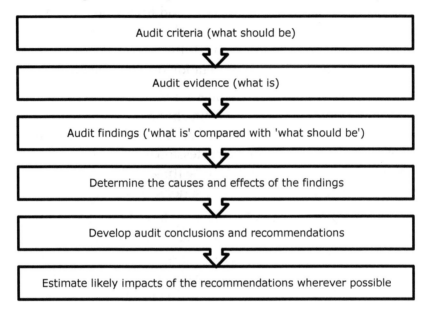

Figure 24 shows the audit/inspection process. The Inspect stage gathers the evidence of 'what is' to compare with the criteria of 'what should be'. Although collecting evidence is central, the relationships formed in the first meeting are vital support to the process.

First Meeting

The relationship between the regulator and those they regulate is instrumental in creating compliance (Ayres and Braithwaite, 1992). Observations of inspections and audits reveal the importance of dialogue in communicating regulatory information (Hutter, 1997). For example, the standards used may necessitate interpretation on what exactly is required.

Observations of inspections in care homes for older people (Brady, 2010) revealed the importance of the first meeting between the regulator and the regulated. Relationships were established or renewed and there was extensive communication around the professional principles and values of caring. Ehren et al. (2014) refer to this as 'setting expectations', an important driver for change in the organisations' practices.

Besides setting expectations, the first meeting introduces the inspection/audit plan together with any issues from the previous inspection and any changes to regulatory rules or procedures. For the organisation being regulated, it may mean changes in their organisation, standards or individual circumstances. The first meeting should clarify:

- Who, in the organisation, will be involved
- Where, in the organisation, observation will be taking place
- The timescale of the inspection or audit
- When and where feedback will take place and the frequency of any intermediate feedback
- The process of completing the report, if there is one
- Opportunities to comment and to reply.

Often the organisation being audited/inspected arranges a contact person. This is helpful in clarifying and delegating responsibility for:

- Conveying information to management
- Acting as an intermediary in arranging contacts within the organisation (Swedish National Audit Office, 2012).

> Apply to your work
>
> Reflect on one of your recent 'first meetings'. In what ways do you 'set expectations'?

Procedural Justice

One of the most important characteristics valued by those inspected is that the inspection is fair and that the inspector is fair, open and transparent (Nursing Homes Ireland, 2010, Tyler, 2006). 'Procedural justice' is a term referring to:

- The perceived fairness of procedures involved in decision-making and
- The perceived treatment one receives from the decision-maker.

In other words, it relates to how a person may perceive the interpersonal treatment they have received from an authority, regardless of whether the resulting outcome will be favourable or not. Research into the effects of procedural justice has consistently found that people and organizations are much more likely to obey the law and accept decisions made by authorities when they feel that the decision-making procedures are fair, respectful, and impartial They are also more likely to report wrongdoing to an authority that has treated them fairly (Murphy et al., 2009: p. 2).

Research implies that using *procedural justice* makes individuals more likely to comply with the decisions of regulators and other legal bodies (Murphy et al., 2009, Tyler, 2003) even where those decisions are unfavourable.

Principles of procedural justice include:

- That decision-making is based on discernible objective evidence
- That the actions of the regulators are understandable and clear
- That people are treated with dignity and fairness
- That people have the opportunity to state their point of view (Murphy et al., 2009).

The principles outlined above should set the boundaries of the relationship being offered.

If the 'Pyramid Planning' model (Minto, 1987) is considered useful, as referred to in Chapter 4, a copy of the inspection/audit plan should be provided to the regulated body. This can help demonstrate the transparency and fairness of the regulation and audit processes and serve to clarify any misunderstandings. Your emphasis on the principles, beliefs and values of the regulated sector, together with the fairness of procedural justice, gives firm boundaries to the relationships in the regulatory interaction.

> Apply to your work
>
> The procedural justice approach emphasises the importance of interpersonal relationships. Would this approach be useful in your work? If so, how?

Implementing the Inspection/audit Plan

The Inspection/audit plan should be sufficiently flexible to accommodate unexpected evidence that reveals new ways of understanding the organisation's performance. Data-collection may support the choice of main questions or raise contradictory issues and fresh points of view.

Figure 25: The Process of Data Becoming Evidence

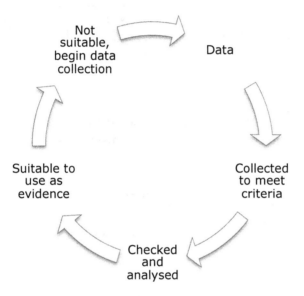

Data may not be suitable for a range of reasons. There are four conditions necessary for data to become evidence:

- It must be fair and, as far as possible, free from bias
- It must reflect the individual circumstances
- It must have the capacity to indicate either intentionality, reasons, knowledge, beliefs or probability
- It must relate to a particular fact in question.

Figure 26: Choosing Information-collection Methods

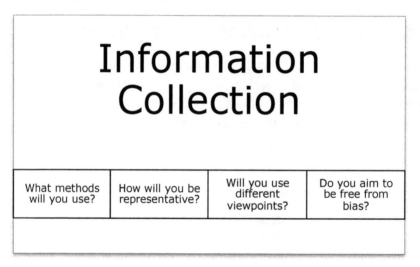

Collecting high quality information poses choices around methods, representativeness, authenticity and freedom from bias. It also requires taking a critical attitude to sources.

Take a Critical Attitude to all Sources

The Swedish National Audit Office recommends a 'source critical attitude' to all data-collection:

> When we collect quantitative data from auditees or agencies that specifically provide data, we should always acquire knowledge about the quality of that data. When we pose questions to persons in interviews or through questionnaires, we should reflect on the credibility of their answers. Credibility may decrease if the person has an interest in influencing opinion in a certain direction or if there is dependence involved in his or her role. In interviews, it is always good to pose follow-up questions about how various details can be substantiated, for example if there is written documentation (reports, statistics, etc.) that provides evidence of what the person is saying (Swedish National Audit Office, 2012: p. 51).

Taking a critical attitude, checking one's own bias, anticipating inspection risks and problems are important to ensure information of the highest possible quality is collected. We deal with this more fully at the end of the chapter.

We now move on to discussing the advantages and disadvantages of each information-collection method and how to use them. Although introducing them here one at a time, one of the strengths of these methods is in combining them.

> Apply to your work
>
> In what ways do you take a 'critical attitude' to the information sources you use?

Different Information-collection Methods

Figure 27: Information-collection Methods

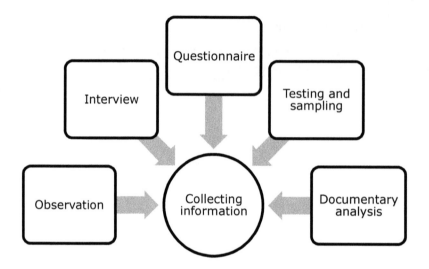

We now consider each information-collection method in turn.

Interviews

An important mode of collecting information is the interview. Here we define the interview as ranging from simply talking to people to the formal interview under caution. The regulator should expect varied demands in the interview situation. Your organisation may have guidance on interviewing and particular restrictions on type, subject and location.

It is usual for research interviewing to use closed questions. This means there is only a restricted choice of answer and that the questions chosen avoid leading the interviewee.

Figure 28: Five Stages of Interviewing (adapted from EPA, 2002)

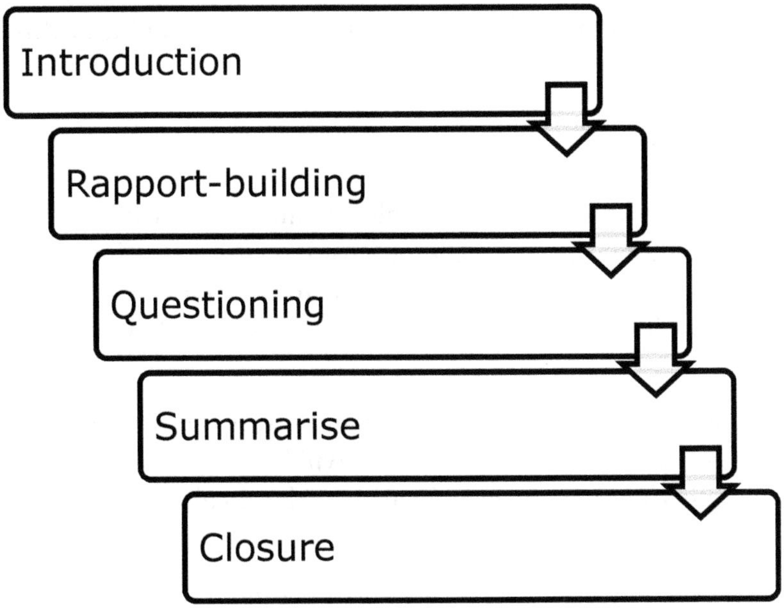

However, a research-based model is not a good fit in a regulatory context. Academic research techniques are concerned with the degree to which results might be generally significant. Because inspection focuses on specific performance and the possible infringement of rules, there is less emphasis on generalizability. For that reason, an inspection/audit interview will make more use of open-ended questions.

Introduction

No matter how informal the interview might be, the inspector should introduce himself or herself showing identification and stating why they wish to speak with that person. Stating the aims of the interview is of great importance in persuading potential interviewees to take part.

The inspector should carry a notebook but should endeavour not to use it until later in the interview. Details can be discussed when the interviewee is more relaxed and forthcoming but noting the person's name and position within the organisation is essential. The ideal circumstances for an interview - quiet, relaxed, etc. - are not always achievable.

Rapport-building

Rapport begins as soon as you meet the interviewee. Letting that person introduce themselves is a good way to build rapport. Do not hurry this stage.

Questioning

Questions should be kept clear and simple and ambiguities avoided. Sensitive or difficult questions should be saved to later in the interview. It may be helpful to put questions first that give an orientation to the organisation, how it works. This calms the interviewee and provides useful information.

Difficult language, such as technical terms and acronyms, should be avoided. Instead, use terms the interviewee will be familiar with. Questions that lead the interviewee into a certain answer should also be avoided, such as –

Did you see that all the guards were off the machine?

Similarly, avoid negative questions such as:

You don't know what time this happened, do you?

The expected answer is obviously a 'no'.

Avoid compound questions (more than one question at the same time), which may be either confusing for the interviewee or may result in their answering only the last question they hear. Similarly, highly complex questions should be avoided – they are difficult to follow and to answer.

Inspection interviews tend to use open-ended questions that allow people to talk about situations and events in their own words. This type of questioning often begins with 'Tell me about ... or uses the W5H questions, Who, What, Where, When, Why and How.

Using this question type allows the interviewer to:

- Learn more about the person
- Reveal facts that you were not aware of
- Relax the interviewee and let them feel in control
- Enable the interviewer to bring out the emotional context of situations and events
- Gives the interviewer time to ask more questions based on the content of the previous answer.

The downside is that the answers may be misleading and time-consuming; the interviewee may be hoping to talk until time runs out. Close-ended questions can then be used to get exact detail. Whether auditing or inspecting alone or in a team, it is useful to build an interview guide related to the evidence your plan identified. Sharing this with the inspection/audit team supports consistency and enables a more efficient division of work amongst colleagues.

The Roles of Interviewees

Different interviewees will have different organisational roles. Some will be experts, some stakeholders and others will be operational members of the organisation. For each role, different styles of question could be relevant. The table below gives an idea of the types of question available:

Table 6: Different Questions for Different Data

Style of question	Example
Knowledge-based question	When was the grant awarded?
Time-frame-based question	What was the previous system of control?
Opinion-based question	Do you think that the present frequency of examination is the right one?
Feelings-based question	Do you feel comfortable about the arrangements for internal audit?
Sensory-based question	What do you see when you work with Team X?
Experience-based question	What is your background?
Behaviour-based question	What happens when there is a spillage?

Listening is important; the interviewer should not be talking more than the interviewee. It is important to show interest, however, using eye contact, head nods, smiles and one-word agreements.

In some regulatory interviews, the expectation is that the interviewer incorporates feedback and educational content. Greenfield et al. (2008) explored the styles that interviewers used to structure feedback to those interviewed in an accreditation event.

The Summary Phase of the Interview

Summarising allows the interviewee to confirm the interviewer's understanding of the information. A single interviewer should take notes at this time, as doing so earlier may prove a distraction. State the important details in proper sequence. The interviewee should be asked to verify and correct any discrepancies.

Closure

The interviewer should manage the emotions of the interview and the expectations of change brought about by their intervention. As the interview is closing, thank the interviewee for their cooperation and/or empathise with the difficulty they may have had in cooperating. Reassure on the confidential nature of the interview and exchange contact details should the interviewee wish to add any detail in the future.

Cognitive Interviewing

The cognitive interview is drawn from social psychology (see Fisher and Geiselman, 2010) and its design compensates for the rational, impersonal approach of most interviews. A core principle of this technique is sensitivity to the interviewee's emotions and recollections. It is suitable for witnesses and victims of an inappropriate practise or culture. It is not a template for an interview. On the contrary, it is a very flexible means of achieving two ends:

- Eliciting as much information as is possible from the interview especially where the witness or informant may only offer a partial recollection of the events
- Controlling and expanding the means of communication, for example through probing and thinking aloud in order to invoke memory recall.

Below are some of the key stages of the cognitive interview:

- Control anxiety and develop rapport
- Ask the interviewee to volunteer information and not to edit thoughts
- Value the interviewee for the information provided
- Request a narrative
- Allow the interviewee to speak without interruption
- Probe the narrative
- Review the interview and confirm and/or explore new details
- Close the interview and attend to background information not directly relevant such as phone numbers etc. Ask the interviewee to call if there is more information remembered.

This technique is helpful in focusing on the emotional situation of the interviewee in order to aid recollection. It requires good listening skills and uses strategies to help people remember the details of their complaint or experience. It is not, however, appropriate for every interview especially where closed questions are required to establish facts.

Social Influence and the Interview

The interview is also subject to social pressures:

- Perceptions of the interviewer as powerful and having legal authority may influence the interviewee (Kvale, 2006)
- The interview may be a two-way struggle as the interviewee can withhold information and/or seek to change the perception of the interviewer. Unstructured interviews are more likely to see interviewee control strategies (Vähäsantanen and Saarinen, 2013). The interviewee may wish to find out who the complainant was or how strong the regulator's stance is on following-up on non-compliance.

Follow-up Questions

Follow-up questions probe where previous answers suggest scope for further inquiry. They can also clarify a vague response.

- Ask the question again, using different words or emphasis to aid clarity
- The implications of answers can be explored e.g. the interviewee might give 'safe' answers – 'I'm only the widget moulder' – so a follow-up is required
- Beware of asking leading questions e.g. *'Do you have any problems with the manager?'* This suggests to the interviewee that there are problems where there may be none. To avoid a leading question, *'Tell me about your relationship with your manager'* is preferable. Leading questions will undermine your conclusions.

> Apply to your work
>
> Look back at the interview section: in what ways could you improve your interview skills?

Criminal Offences and Evidence

The regulator may encounter criminal violations in the course of information-collection. If inspecting using a legislative framework that includes criminal offences, the information collected may be used as evidence in a prosecution. Interviews will need to fit with national and organisational guidance on criminal evidence (for example, in the UK it is the Police and Criminal Evidence Act 1984). Interview skills should be suitably flexible for interviewing non-violating persons as well as whistleblowers or victims of the organisation's actions.

Summarising and Interpreting the Interview Data

At the end of an interview, regulatory personnel, including the interviewer and colleagues, will need to draw-out the major themes. If the same questions have been asked of each individual, the responses can be summarised, analysed, compared and contrasted.

The information can be analysed using the following steps:

- Put all of your interview data into Word or a similar programme
- Make a list of the key words from your audit/inspection plan and search using Find. Note the number of occurrences and the context. Which are the most frequent?
- Look at the key questions – how have these been answered?
- Categorise responses into positive/negative/neutral
- Use the software's highlighter tool to mark-up key phrases
- Look for local terms that the interviewees use
- Compare and contrast responses.

> Apply to your work
>
> What method do you use to analyse your interviews?
> How do colleagues analyse interviews?

Strengths and weaknesses of interviews and interview techniques

Table 7: Strengths and Weaknesses of Interviews (ECA, 2013a)

	Strengths	**Weaknesses**
Interviews in general	Are more personal and can elicit more in-depth responses than a questionnaire. Can gather data on various complex issues in an efficient way. Interviews take into account situational and individual factors	The evidence gathered needs to be confirmed by other sources. Can be difficult to draw general conclusions
Unstructured interview	Useful for theory building. May result in more detailed data. Well suited to complex subjects	Can be time-intensive. Additional effort involved in data analysis. Difficult to quantify data
Structured interview	Useful for hypothesis testing. Generates breadth of data. More easily quantified	Limited options can cause bias in responses. Need very good advance knowledge. May make it difficult to reach a more in-depth understanding

Observation

Using observation to collect information is a method often synonymous with the 'walk-through' but there is a lot more to it than simply walking through. Being on-site means that the auditor or inspector can crosscheck the information obtained at interview with what is encountered in plain sight.

Observation is a method of collecting data on events, a physical setting or a person's behaviour. The advantages of observation are:

- Data can be collected at the exact time an event is occurring, for example in the areas of manufacturing, care or food-preparation
- It does not depend on people's willingness or capacity to supply information
- Observation can be unobtrusive as personnel may not even be aware that data is being collected
- Observation can record what is not happening, such as safety measures that are ignored
- It can record intended and unintended consequences.

There are also disadvantages:

- Being observed may alter a person's behaviour, especially where the observation is deliberately apparent and obtrusive
- There is a likelihood that physical settings may have been modified in anticipation of the observation
- Observer bias – the observer may be selective in what is observed or interpret what is seen to support their own point of view.

Observation can be overt or covert (the following section draws on CDC, 2008b). Inspection typically uses overt observation but there are situations in which covert observation is justified, for example, when monitoring the hours a business is selling alcohol. Such covert surveillance may require special permission.

Observation may also be direct or indirect. Direct observation could be an auditor watching employee interactions and behaviours as they occur. In contrast, indirect observation would be watching the results of interactions and behaviours where these behaviours are difficult to see directly, as with soil disturbance after nuclear testing or observing signs of pest activity – cockroach droppings in a kitchen, for example.

Additionally, observation may be used:

- When trying to comprehend a process or the forms of management control around that process
- When focusing on critical processes such as reception in an emergency ward or staff changeovers in a nursing home
- When determining how people work together or how a person or number of people behave
- When evaluating the state of physical surroundings, equipment, layout or facilities
- For whatever reason people are unable to supply information.

Structured Observation

A research-based approach would include a structured observation schedule (Bryman, 2004) of, possibly, an observation every ten minutes. The Short Observation Framework for Inspection (SOFI) is a structured observation record developed specifically for inspection use by the UK Bradford Dementia Group. It requires a two-hour observation of people with dementia focusing on behaviour to indicate mood, emotion, engagement and staff interaction. The tool is **not** used alone but with other evidence.

Not all observation is as structured but maintaining a clear focus for the observation is necessary to record and analyse what you are seeing. That focus can be on:

- An individual or group
- Scanning the behaviour of a group of individuals
- Having a checklist of equipment to scan and check
- Using indirect observation, as in recording effluent discharge in a waterway.

Video Surveillance

A further form of observation is video surveillance. Covert video filming has been successful in care and animal industries to expose cruelty and neglect. These have triggered inspections of facilities and regulatory and legal sanctions. Regulators have also used covert surveillance in

- Illegal sales to minors

- Breaking the conditions of a licence

- The illegal dumping of waste.

Where regulators conduct such surveillance, there is specific guidance on the use of unmarked cars, video equipment, cameras and binoculars. A notebook records diagrams, maps and information such as the time of day.

Although observation can reveal many things, it is often difficult to impute meaning or intention from an observation. To confirm these, the regulator would need to use other methods such as the interview. Where observation detects violations but there has not been the opportunity to interview, the regulator may not have the power to obtain identification or to search - police involvement may be necessary.

Testing and Analysis

Testing materials to ascertain soundness, quality and condition is an established activity of many inspection/audits.

Pharmaceutical regulators, for example, routinely test medical ingredients for quality; there are routine tests on water quality and effluent levels. Health and social care regulators may test water temperature and room sizes.

Testing of structures and materials is also a core part of many inspection activities, especially in the oil and aviation and the food industries, with supporting standards and guidance (API, 2009).

Collecting Information from Documents

In general, working documents, electronic or otherwise, of an organisation will contain the following information:

- The structure of its governance
- Hierarchies of accountability
- Records and notifications that must be kept for regulatory purposes such as accidents and death
- Documents from suppliers showing the origins and manufacturing guarantees of raw materials and supplies including certificates of manufacturing quality specific to the sector
- Financial documents, invoices and receipts kept for audit
- Documents detailing the risk and safety management arrangements and controls such as Standard Operating Procedures (SOPs) - in some cases this will include cleaning records
- Documents may include logs, performance ratings, funding proposals, minutes of meetings, newsletters and marketing materials (CDC, 2009).

This not an exhaustive list - the quantity of documentation can often overwhelm! Most documentation, however, is now in a digital format and can be easily provided *before* an inspection. Some regulators state that they prefer only working documents and add that documents specifically prepared for the event should be avoided. Although such caution is understandable, using summary documents reduces the amount of time spent going through large amounts of records; an inspector with doubts should crosscheck with a sample of the original records.

Documents should contain information relevant to your inspection/audit and should:

- Record the up-to-date policies of the organisation in line with the requirements of the standards
- Communicate standard operating procedures (SOPs), record adverse events and consequent actions, machinery maintenance, operator working times etc. Documents are essential in the control of risk and other hazards. It is arguable that without systematic and updated documentation (or its digital equivalent) a risk and safety system cannot be maintained

- Provide data for further analysis such as number, type and origins of recipients of a service
- Provide background information – documents that set out the aims, mission and values of the organisation
- Provide planning and managing information-collection through documents.

The range of documents made available should be assessed and cross-referenced with evidence-collection criteria. Which documents will answer queries and provide evidence? Is there a critical process where examination of documents is essential?

Before an announced visit, the organization should be notified of the documents required for scrutiny. Document examination should be limited to those identified as relevant to your inspection/audit criteria. If possible and time allowing, producers of the documents should be consulted so as to understand its original purpose. Document accuracy should be determined – speaking to the original writers, if possible, will help here.

It may be beneficial to create a means of summarizing data gathered from the documents into whatever form your organisation uses. Some regulators use a standard form to summarize and answer each of the evidence-collection criteria (CDC, 2009).

Why Bother with Documents?

Regulators are aware that the inspection of documents is time-consuming and gives the impression that the regulator never meets consumers or those on the shop floor.

Hood and Peters (2004) argue that increased regulation tends to distract middle and upper-level officials, creates massive paperwork and produces major unintended effects'. The concern is that the intention of inspection is to focus attention on process and procedures and away from outcome to the extent that senior managers become overly obsessed with 'Key Performance Indicators' (Munro, 2004) and the documentation perceived as evidencing them.

At the same time, there are concerns over the validity of some documentation (remember our example of hospital waiting lists in Chapter 4); in terms of not only its authenticity but also that it presents a 'creative compliance' view of the organisation's performance.

However, while the above are significant criticisms of trends and tendencies in regulation, we need to remember the advantages that judicious use of documentary information offers:

- Policy and governance documents hold organisations to account for their aims and values. They are evidence of the intent of the organisation
- Policy documents reveal risk-management controls, enabling the cross-checking of documents and procedures with the behaviour and views of staff
- Internal and external audit documents can be useful but will probably need confirmatory checks (a source-critical attitude).

Apply to your own Work

Drawing on your own experience, consider how document quality has contributed to or detracted from inspection/audit outcomes.

Questionnaires

A questionnaire is a prepared set of questions intended for face-to-face, telephone, postal mail, email or Internet use. Some regulators and agencies make strong suggestions on the questions to use. Regulators often issue a pre-existing questionnaire to staff or those using the inspected organization. Alternatively, they may design a specific questionnaire for the organisation. Questionnaires administered outside a face-to-face environment may include:

- General intelligence gathering such as the UK National Health Service/Care Quality Commission patient survey (but see also Aiken et al., 2012)
- Surveys of groups that would be too large to interview individually, such as a large organisation's employees
- Surveys of those who are difficult to contact in working hours or where they are dispersed (home workers).

The strengths of the questionnaire include:

- Enabling anonymous responses where sensitive information is involved
- Useful where resources are limited
- Can reach a larger number of people
- Can reflect attitudes and bias.

Disadvantages include:

- Language difficulties
- Alienation of those with difficulty with the written language or where English is not the first language
- Low response rates are normal for questionnaires.

Planning Your Questionnaire

Set Objectives

The audit/inspection plan will provide the questionnaire objectives.

Select the Number and Type of Participants

The objectives determine the nature of participant for the questionnaire i.e. for the effectiveness of a new training course; for example, the questionnaire will target those who undertook that course.

Selecting the number of participants can depend on resources, on the numbers of relevant people or a combination of both. For example, if only 20 people take a training course, they can all be approached but if thousands have done so, it might be necessary to select a sample group.

Ask Clear, Concise Questions

Participants of a questionnaire may be in hurry and/or lacking in enthusiasm so failure to immediately understand the questionnaire will discourage participation.

The Questionnaire Appraisal System (CDC, 2008a) provides a number of checks to design better quality questionnaires:

Anonymity: Should the questionnaire be anonymous or should there be an option for providing contact details? Is this clear in the questionnaire?

Reading: Is any question difficult to read – is the sentence too long, does it contain unnecessarily specialised or technical vocabulary? Are there words of five syllables where two would do?

Missing information: Is there sufficient information in the question to result in a useable answer?

Instructions: Are the instructions conflicting or inaccurate? Would you describe the instructions as complicated, inadequate or useful?

Clarity: Is any question unduly complicated or too vague?

Technical terminology: Is it defined, clear and simply expressed?

Appropriate questions: Do the questions assume knowledge the participants actually have? Do the questions require difficult mental calculations?

Decide whether to use closed, open questions, or a combination of the two. As mentioned earlier in the chapter, closed questions are unambiguous and use pre-determined answers from which to choose. Open questions allow an answer in the participant's own words. They are useful for more insightful, detailed and unexpected information but are more difficult to summarise and categorise making analysis time-consuming and challenging.

Closed questions are much easier to compare and analyse.

Include demographic questions – such as age, sex, race, education and occupation but only if relevant e.g. if all your participants are senior lecturers, then it is unnecessary to ask their occupation.

Order questions appropriately - if a question is sensitive leave it towards the end, start with the less controversial. Aim for a logical order likely to make sense to the participant.

Pilot the questionnaire - don't waste money printing hundreds of questionnaires you later realize to be inappropriate. Test on a small group. If you have followed the design principles above, pilot testing will reveal any unanticipated problems.

Obtaining an Adequate Response Rate

Higher response rates strengthen your results.

- The purpose and value of the questionnaire should be clearly communicated. The plan for how the data will be used should also be clearly stated, as should how the results will be of use to the participants and/or the wider society
- Follow-up – the more contact with the participants, the higher the response rate. This is particularly true of email where several messages may be required to obtain a response as one email competes with hundreds of others. It is also advisable to ask for the participant's cooperation in receiving follow-up emails to avoid deletion
- A financial incentive or competition prize might increase the response rate but could invite criticism regarding the participant's motivation.

> Apply to your work
>
> What are the advantages and disadvantages of using questionnaires in your work?

Recording Information

It is crucial that information collected is accurately recorded. Unanticipated shortfalls in a process, violations and non-compliance will need recording. Regulators build in frequent breaks to complete notes. Many agencies have standard recording forms and logbooks for observations and interviews. Each inspector/auditor should maintain their own notes but it is permitted in some organisations to initial a colleague's notes if you have been present at the event.

An inspector should use their judgement as to whether notes should be taken during observation, interviews or conversation. Note-taking at the time improves accuracy but it may also prevent a flow of information, intimidate people and cause interviewer and respondent to loose the thread of the questioning. In a research setting, note-taking at the time is discouraged and audiotaping encouraged but again seeing the inspector set-up recording equipment and being on record interferes with the naturalness and possibly the candour of the encounter.

Personal Data

Note-taking, video surveillance, observation and surveys may require collection of personal data such as email or postal address. You will need to check with your organisation on issues and procedures in line with your local data protection legislation.

Management of Information 'Off the Record'

People providing information may wish to remain anonymous. This may be because that person is revealing something about which regulatory staff may have been unaware. Awareness of the relevant whistleblowing legislation (see chapter 4) is necessary. This information should be kept separately from the main records of the inspection/audit any off-the-record information. It is important to protect anonymity (Swedish National Audit Office, 2012).

Using Contemporaneous Notes

Records in a notebook are collected in a specific and methodical way in order to provide sound evidence. This method is known as keeping 'Contemporaneous Notes'. They are made as soon after an information-collection event as possible. Good contemporaneous notes are complete and accurate, assist in writing the report and contribute to an accurate statement suitable for court. They should contain:

- The location
- Names of people involved/present
- Date, duration and time of the event
- Advice normally adds they should be as detailed as possible
- Indexed if possible.

The UK Home Office adds the following strictures for the use of official notebooks that may help those of you not familiar with the contemporaneous notebook:

When to Use a Separate Page

You must use a separate page for each:

- Surveillance period
- Operation
- Task
- Incident.

Blank spaces and deletions:

- Rule through, sign, date and time blank spaces at the end of a series of entries, and
- Make deletions with a single line, initialled and dated.

Do not:

- Leave blank spaces between words or any lines left between entries
- Use correction fluid or other types of erasing products, and
- Rub out mistakes with an eraser or strike through deletions in heavy pen (Home Office, 2014: p. 11).

All notes should be as unbiased as possible and factual with no derogatory comments. Photographs or removal of items to use as evidence should also be recorded (date, time, location, method) (Interior Health, 2008).

Research on contemporaneous note-taking is restricted to police officers but illustrates the difficulties encountered and skills needed. Gregory et al (2011) found that police officer contemporaneous note taking is accurate but incomplete. Respondents missed out 68% of witness information and failed to include interview questions. A study by Powell et al (2011) confirmed these findings and went on to consider how to improve contemporaneous note-taking. It was found that question codes, layout styles that separate questions and responses and the use of abbreviations improved the range of information recorded. The above suggests skill, training and practice are needed for contemporaneous note-taking to be an effective tool in supporting memory and accuracy.

> Apply to your work
>
> Do you encounter difficulty with contemporaneous note taking? How might you improve your skills?

Digital Programmes for Information-collection

Digital programmes (trade names are 'Casenotes' and 'Lima') that date stamp and track changes to typed-up notes and which also incorporate voice, photography and video recording can be installed on smartphones and tablets and are therefore portable. They satisfy all of the evidential quality of the hand written contemporaneous note. These may not be appropriate in all inspection scenarios but do illustrate how a difficult skill can be supported.

These programmes also offer a means of managing and syncing note-taking. The volume of notes generated through inspection is large and one of the skills needed is accurate note-taking for generating accurate reports. Nevertheless, the handwritten note is still required in some jurisdictions together with strong organisational control over issue, quality, storage and retrieval (Home Office, 2014).

Digital technology also applies to the inspection/audit process using handheld digital devices such as scanners, cameras, smartphones and tablets. Standards and violations can be ticked off on screen. There is little research on this area:

For restaurant hygiene inspections, the state of Florida has introduced a handheld electronic device, the Portable Digital Assistant (PDA), which reminds inspectors of about 1,000 potential violations that may be checked for. Using administrative data on inspections conducted from July 2003 to June 2009, the adoption of PDAs led to 11% more detected violations. Subsequently, restaurants increased their compliance efforts, but the response was gradual. Nevertheless, the heightened compliance induced by PDA use has contributed to reducing the risk of restaurant-related foodborne disease outbreaks (Jin and Lee, 2013: p. 3).

Witness Statements

If an allegation is made of an activity you think potentially criminal, the inspector must provide evidence that will stand-up in a court of law in the form of a 'witness statement'. It will also be necessary to contact the police. The inspector should refer to the organisation's instructions regarding the witness statement.

A witness statement can be defined as:

A document recording the evidence of a person, which is signed, by that person to confirm that the content of the statement is true.

Guidance on Compiling a Witness Statement

- It is essential that the interviewee understand the implications of giving his/her information. It must be established **at the start** that the interviewee is prepared to give information in the form of a signed statement that may be used later at a trial or formal enquiry
- The interviewees' name, address, place of work, work address and their job title should be included in their statement
- The statement should be clear, detailed and, where possible, concise
- The statement should cover all relevant information pertaining to the potentially criminal activity:
    - Time, even if approximate
    - Date
    - The event as witnessed in sequential order
    - If relevant, who was present?
    - If relevant, who did what, where and to whom?
- The statement should contain facts, not opinions. Exceptions to this include where the interviewee's opinion would be considered 'expert', such as a doctor or fire officer
- Hearsay should be avoided. Hearsay is evidence based on the reports of others rather than something personally witnessed by the

interviewee
- Where there are gaps or inconsistencies in the interviewee's account, reasons should be provided
- Open-ended questions should be used at first e.g. 'What happened?'
- They should be followed by more detailed questions when the interviewee appears more relaxed
- A first-person narrative should be used, e.g. 'I saw this', 'I did this' and the interviewees' words should be transcribed accurately
- Interviewees provide the most detailed recall if handled with sensitivity so it is important to:
  - Maintain eye contact
  - Maintain equal terms – sit at the same height, avoid sitting behind a desk
  - Focus on the speaker
  - Nod the head
  - Avoid interrupting, where possible
- The interviewee should print and sign their name and date the document stating in writing that it is a true and accurate statement
- The interviewer should give the interviewee their name and contact details, should they wish to change or add to their statement later or have any questions.

High Quality Information

The inspector should do their utmost to ensure that information-collection methods:

- Avoid bias
- Are accurate.

Avoiding Bias

Information-collection is biased when it supports the view of only one party or is selected to support only a specific argument.

Understanding the organisation accurately requires the collection of representative information. To avoid bias, it may be useful to select informants at random or to devise a quota so that information is being drawn from representative strata of the organisation.

Information may become biased by:

- Not including a range of staff, customers and managers
- Leaving important individuals or groups out because they are difficult to access
- Unintentionally excluding those who have little communication abilities, dementia or learning difficulties
- In the case of a proxy representative, for example family, parents or carers, views of the proxy may be different from those of the person they are representing. If they do differ, it is worth considering if these views are legitimate
- Where there are inspection problems such as data ambiguity, poor data, creative compliance, resistance or regulatory capture
- Questions including preconceived assumptions or emotive phrases.

Figure 29: Triangulation and Checking Sources

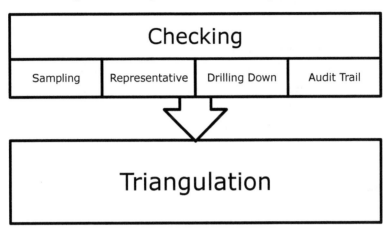

Combining Methods: Triangulation

We have discussed information-collection methods as if they were stand-alone, or with the assumption that using one prevented the use of another. The reality is that these methods are more powerful when used in combination. **Triangulation** is the practice of combining different points of view on an issue, subject or person. We discussed triangulation briefly in the planning chapter (Chapter 4). Differing sources of information on the same thing or event give greater accuracy and insight.

The following are examples of triangulation concentrating on safety:

- Using documents to audit the extent and robustness of safety measures
- Testing or sampling the soundness and maintenance of safety equipment and materials
- Conducting an anonymous questionnaire survey of the workforce to determine their views on safety issues
- Interviewing management and union representatives and their families to see how far they confirmed, denied or offered completely new perspectives on an issue
- Observing and interviewing people looking for confirmation or contradiction
- Interviewing people at different levels of the organization.

All forms of information-collection can triangulate against each other or within themselves (viz. looking at documents from different locations and levels of the organisation (Jick, 1979).

Using Triangulation also enables crosschecking across modes of information-collection. Triangulation can be carried out horizontally, for example, via interviews with heads of departments or vertically by looking at the Quality Management and Safety policies, tracking their implementation down to the shop floor by interviewing individual operatives. Triangulation can also be achieved by collecting information at different times.

Drilling Down

There are two definitions of 'drilling down'. The first is to establish root causes and is another way of describing 'Root Cause Analysis', as discussed in Chapter 3.

The second defines it as getting detailed information from top-level documents on policy and then 'drilling down' using interviews, observation and records to see just how that policy is working 'on the shop floor'. This is important for risk-based inspection where it is crucial to understand the organisation's risk-assessment, management and control systems.

Case-tracking and Audit Trails

'Case-tracking' is when an individual person or product, is tracked through the processes and procedures used by the organisation. This is very useful for gaining new insights into the consumer experience. For example, a hospital may correctly view its processes as medical and administrative and of high quality but the experience for the patient can be very different. Patients may have uncertainties about why they are attending hospital; they may have to wait many weeks to see a specialist and may come away with little, or inexplicable, information on their condition. The 'Quality Audit Trail' is a technique for tracking exactly what an individual experiences in their contact with an organisation. Tracking a case, taking an individual or number of individuals and examining their experience through interviews, documents and observation, is a valuable tool, giving insights into the impact of the process on the individual as well as the impact of outputs.

Maintaining a Critical Attitude to Your Sources

Information supplied by the organisation will need to be confirmed. We have already discussed the use of observation to confirm interview findings. Techniques such as triangulation, drilling down, audit trails and case-tracking are further means of maintaining a critical attitude to sources without becoming unfair.

> Apply to your work
>
> What methods do you use to confirm the information supplied to you?

Interpreting Evidence

Figure 30: Interpreting Evidence

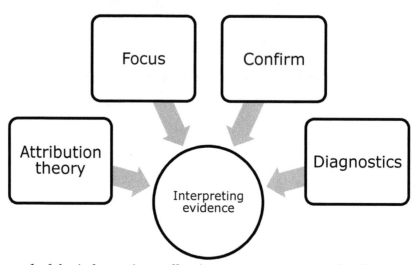

At the end of the information-collection stage, an organized collection of interviews, statements, observations, tests and questionnaire responses or a mixture of the above will exist, one that examines the main questions from a number of perspectives. It must be ensured that any third party cannot tamper with evidence. The previous section looked at ways to ensure the quality of information-collection. This one determines which is the best evidence and if more information is required via drilling down, triangulation, case study or audit trail. Conferring with colleagues and pooling information may be required.

At this stage, information should be assessed and a decision made as to what degree it establishes fact. Have collection methods compromised the data? It must be as fair and as free from bias as possible to:

- Reflect the individual circumstances
- Indicate intentionality, reasons, knowledge, beliefs or probability
- Relate to a particular fact in question
- Be sufficient, relevant and reliable
- Answer the main question(s) of your inspection/audit plan
- Raise new questions
- Pinpoint omissions and gaps.

When collection methods and the quantity and quality of your evidence are deemed satisfactory, there are a number of conceptual tools to help with further interpretation of your information.

Attribution

Attribution theories represent a social-psychological contribution to understanding how people make sense of and explain behaviour and regulators are not immune to these processes. In attribution theories, a distinction is made between:

- The actor – the person demonstrating the behaviour, and
- The observer - the person observing the behaviour.

Both can explain the behaviour. Firstly, a judgement is made as to whether the behaviour is intentional or unintentional. Consequently, the actor may explain the behaviour in terms of external influences or his or her own reasoning and beliefs. The observer tends to explain the behaviour in terms of the internal beliefs and reasons of the actor. This culminates in the allocation of blame.

'The owner should have put the dog on a lead, then it wouldn't have bitten the child'

Actors and observers tend to put forward different explanations for behaviour and its intentionality. They may act immediately on these assumptions and proceed to lay blame or they may try to test them out by getting more information.

Attribution theories, tentative as they are (Malle, 2011), give regulators cautionary insight into the need for evidence and discussion before attributing intentionality, reasons, beliefs and blame. A regulator may want to review:

- If any other factors may have influenced these results?
- If this particular organisation is unique in some respect?
- If the customer/user-base is unique in some way?
- If there are there other factors outside the control of the organisation?

> Apply to your work
>
> Is there an example from your work that displays the
> insights of attribution theory?

Interpreting Data – Confirming Evidence

At this point, the inspector should fine-tune evidence to determine that it
meets inspection/audit evidence criteria. An early task should be ensuring
that your information is in a manageable form. It may already be indexed
or related to specific issues or standards but it may also be necessary to
draw together the data from colleagues.

Maintain Your Plan

The main question(s) selected from the dominant issues guides the
investigation but new facts revealed through the inspection may prompt an
expansion or narrowing of scrutiny.

Is the data of sufficient quality to make sound evidence? Photographs,
video and audio recording prove a fact in the same way as signed and
witnessed statements. The quality of 'hard evidence', such as photos, video
and audio, may need to be improved or enhanced to stand as evidence.

Qualitative Data

Most data will be qualitative, i.e. in a non-numeric form. It will include
contemporaneous notes, transcripts, observation notes, diagrams, maps
and digital recordings. They may represent a huge quantity of information
that is time-consuming but necessary. As the data is evaluated as evidence,
it is also interpreted – attaching meaning and significance to it. In so
doing, the inspector should try to draw out themes and issues and to find
any *relationships* that exist between those themes and issues. If a gap is
found in data, it may be necessary to collect more. Constantly interpreting
and evaluating reduces the need for this, but also creates the risk of
premature interpretation. Again, the key factor is careful initial planning.

Quantitative Data

A proportion of the data collected will also be quantitative and will depend
on the industry involved and methods of data-collection. Quantitative data

is numeric - it is statistical analysis that compares and summarizes. There are a number of useful and visual quantitative tools such as:

- Frequency graphs and bar charts
- Percentages as used in pie charts
- Ratios showing the relationship between two groups, for example, students and lecturers or doctors and patients
- Finally, there is the average (mean, median, mode), which is often the basis of 'Key Performance Indicators'.

Meeting the Standard of Proof

Two terms assist understanding of the legal aspects of evidence. The 'burden of proof' is a term used across jurisdictions. In the main, the burden of proving either a criminal or civil violation lies with the organisation or person to prove its allegations. Acting with your organisation, the inspector must be able to prove an allegation. In the context of this discussion the quality of evidence will play a crucial role in backing-up an allegation.

However, there are different 'standards of proof'. In the United States, for example, there are several different standards but in the main, we can distinguish, as in the UK, that there is a standard of proof for civil trials that differs from that required for a criminal trial. In a civil trial, the standard of proof is 'on the balance of probabilities', i.e. what is more probably than not. In the criminal environment however, standards are higher and a case must be 'beyond reasonable doubt'. Most violations of regulatory law are civil so the level of proof you are seeking to show is that it is more likely than not.

Apply to your work
What are the standards of proof used in your work?

Analysing the Organisation

No matter how well data is collected and collated, its value is limited if it does not produce an understanding of how the organisation is functioning and for whom.

There are a number of ways to establish the degree to which the criteria have been achieved:

- Compare this organisation with other similar organisations inspected or audited
- Determine if there is demonstration of professional principles, beliefs and values
- Determine what efforts the organisation is making to be compliant and to implement best practice
- Determine the ability level of management – do they understand what is required?
- Look at key performance indicators for the sector
- Determine to what extent are risk-assessment and management controls effective
- Determine if the organisation been cooperative and if the level of cooperation relates to any prior regulatory problems.

> Apply to your work
>
> How are you updating your sector expertise? Compare and contrast with colleagues the resources, the opportunities and the difficulties.

Professional Judgement and Regulation

A final analysis may draw on an inspector's in-depth knowledge of the sector and professional skills. Professional judgement refers to decision-making that reflects key values and principles. Evetts lists these as:

- The importance of trust between the professional and the client
- The analysis of risk
- The use of discretion
- Expert knowledge
- High level of service for client and colleague (Evetts, 2013: p. 782).

There are many sectors, for example schools, where regulatory understanding demands professional judgement (Baxter and Clarke, 2013). Biesta (2007) believes that professional judgement uses principles and values to make complex decisions. Principles and values are paramount over other considerations such as economy and efficiency. The use of punishment in the teaching of children provides an example. The removal of privileges and the use of detention may upset a child sufficiently that they try their best to learn, meaning that their results improve and the school seems to show improvement. However, this approach risks alienating teacher and pupil alike not to mention the implications regarding the child's social development and view of society.

Professional values and the principles of education, of children's rights and human development, override what may be thought of as brutal but effective teaching methods. Regulatory judgements in *all* sectors will often rely on professional principles and values.

The Significance of the Findings

Findings that involve safety, risk, criminal activity or negligence may require immediate responses. In the event of serious deficiencies, action should be undertaken before the end of the inspection/audit. The findings will show where the organisation is working and where it is not and the extent to which it has conformed to or deviated from the criteria identified in your plan.

All data has now been collected, reviewed and interpreted and robust evidence identified. The final stage can now be explored – Improvement.

Chapter Six: Improve

Objectives

After reading this chapter you will be able to:

- Foster improvement
- Plan and deliver the final conference
- Hear the other side's point of view
- Make compliance decisions
- Devise a feedback strategy to stakeholders
- Select enforcement instruments if necessary
- Write an Improvement report
- Structure Follow-up.

Rationale

The Improve stage turns from investigating the performance of the organisation to persuading managers to rectify shortfalls and adopt sustainable improvement strategies. The relationship building that began in the first conference and continued during the inspection comes into prominence.

The Improve stage begins with a meeting presenting findings and conclusions. Structured feedback is essential as is giving management the opportunity to reply. Enforcement strategies, where used, respond to the organisation's level of compliance and performance. The action plan, inspection report, gradings, if any, and follow-up are the tools to lever change.

The inspection/audit plan is as important in this final stage as it was in earlier stages. Figure 31 shows the steps of the improve stage.

Figure 31: Improvement: From Plan to Follow-up

Models of Improvement

Figure 32: Models of Improvement

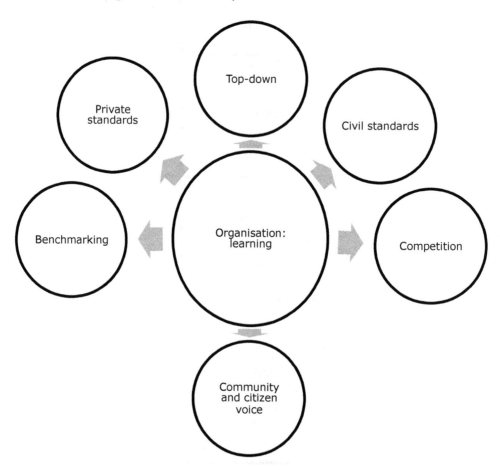

The UK is widely viewed as utilising a 'top-down' regulatory improvement strategy based on key performance indicators of management capacity (Martin et al., 2013). Improvement here is defined by central government and, it is argued, encourages a narrow focus on performance scoring rather than broader outcomes that are of most concern to citizens and service users (Grace and Fenna, 2013).

This top-down model is expanded in the diagram above to include the bottom-up pressures of user/consumer choice and competition. The diagram shows standards bodies and organisational learning, revealing the various bodies with a stake in the organisation's improvement. It also shows external drivers such as competition and benchmarking. The model illustrates the varied ways of achieving improvement rather than relying on one approach.

Brennan and Berwick (1998) identify five ways regulators at street-level can encourage improvement:

- Ensuring compliance with standards and regulations raises quality
- Culling – removing defects from the system by de-licensing or removing accreditation
- Encouraging copying – transferring information and ideas
- Promoting organisational learning
- Fostering creativity – releasing and encouraging regulated organisations to find their own solutions.

Unfortunately, regulation too often relies solely on culling. This tendency, in turn, retards the development of other approaches, as culling often escalates into policing and quality improvement is treated as a matter of removing defects rather than as a continuous process of improving standards or manufacturing better products (Brennan, 1998: p. 712).

Given this tendency towards regulatory culling, it is understandable that improvement is often equated with waiting to hear what the inspector/auditor requires rather than acting on the organization's own initiative (Yapp and Fairman, 2006). A successful strategy to counter this is to stress that the organisation itself has a responsibility for improvement. Naming and shaming, league tables and grading have introduced competition, motivating, in turn, further improvement.

Achieving improvement?

An unintended consequence of top-down regulation, many have argued, has been to discourage innovation and to encourage instead creative compliance (Hood, 2006). Regulated organisations adapt by 'playing-safe', thereby meeting minimum requirements rather than pursuing their own improvement strategies.

Encouraging self-regulation helps achieve the aims of stretched government regulators. The choice by firms of self-regulation is not simply to avoid government regulation; it is to gain advantage in the marketplace. Further, civil and private standards are designed to promote improvement;

there are 94 business excellence awards used in 83 countries (Mohammad et al., 2011). Government regulators can use private standards to exert influence on organisations to improve, reducing their reliance on rules-based regulation as the single mode of persuasion.

What is meant by 'improvement'?

Improvement may be as straightforward as fixing the problems the standards were devised to fix, to sector wide problem solving, or at a micro-level, to the quality of feedback to individuals after accreditation interviews (Greenfield et al., 2008).

Improvement has to be seen not only in terms of financial value but also as improving social value, for example, regulatory objectives seeking better participation by children in care home management. Improvement strategies may also target sustainability, environmental or social responsibility.

Improvement at Street-level

As Braithwaite writes, the financial crisis of 2007/8 did not arrive without warnings from those on the front line:

> With the Global Financial Crisis, as with 9/11, street-level agents again did their job. By 2004 the FBI to its credit reported publicly that it was detecting an epidemic of home loan mortgage fraud. It could hardly fail to notice such a disturbing tsunami of little frauds. By 2006, the Federal Financial Crimes Enforcement Network (FinCEN) reported a 1,411% increase in mortgage-related suspicious activity reports between 1997 and 2005, 66% of which involved material misrepresentation or false documents. Then another 44% increase was reported between 2005 and 2006. Then in 2007, BasePoint Analytics analysed 3 million loans to conclude that 70% of early payment defaults had fraudulent misrepresentations on their original loan applications. Because they were many little frauds, FBI leaders saw them as lower priority matters than other files in their in-trays that might deliver long prison sentences.
> The FBI missed the opportunity to see the big picture of this large pattern of little frauds. They were being sliced and diced,

securitized by Wall Street, and sold off to naive European banks that managed to cripple their economies with the bad debts. Packaged bundles of petty frauds enabled large profits by risk shifting in some cases through major frauds ratcheted upwards by the bonus culture of Wall Street. So the FBI missed the opportunity to save its country from its second major crisis of the 21st century (Braithwaite, 2015: p. 2).

Street-level regulators have a pivotal role identifying emerging problems and hazards and their contribution is central to the improvement of organisations through inspection or audit. Interpersonal skills are essential to communicating the values and principles embedded in the standards and guidance. Ehren called this 'setting expectations' on what constitutes good practice:

inspection primarily drives change indirectly, through encouraging certain developmental processes, rather than through more direct and coercive methods, such as schools reacting to inspection feedback. Specifically, results indicate that school inspections which set clear expectations on what constitutes "good education" for schools and their stakeholders are strong determinants of improvement actions; principals and schools feel pressure to respond to these prompts and improve their education (Ehren et al., 2014: p. 296).

Other strategies such as incorporating feedback in inspections may contribute to challenging intention, ability and motivation.

Improvement then not only relies on the processes and strategies employed by the regulatory body, but crucially on the front-line regulator. Their combination of interpersonal and professional skills are every bit as essential to safeguarding the public good.

The Regulation Relationship

For both the regulator and the regulated, there is mutual gain in managing the relationship. Regulators want to see sustainable self-regulation; regulated organisations have a business interest in maintaining compliance with sector standards. Nevertheless, research supports the ambivalence of the relationship.

Uncertainty Regarding Regulator Action

Regulator and regulated may be unclear about the other's actions and intentions (Etienne, 2013, Hutter, 1997, Saunders et al., 2010, May and Wood, 2003) leading to ambiguity and misunderstanding. Further, various studies (Jin and Lee, 2010, Feinstein, 1989, Mascini and Wijk, 2009) challenge the consistency of regulator actions:

> Inspectors are not automatically able to determine what the right approach is in specific instances and differ significantly in their task definitions (Mascini and Wijk, 2009: p. 33).

May and Wood (2003) found that enforcement styles varied amongst regulators to the point where the regulated did not gain a clear understanding of what was asked of them. The causes of this inconsistency have been found to rest with the regulatory body. Paired with confusing methodologies, aims and measurements, regulators struggle to implement these poorly targeted standards (Walshe and Phipps, 2013).

Given the above, the inspection/audit plan and the main questions will help to ensure continuity and clarity throughout the inspection. Evidence-checking and interpretation in the Inspect stage prepare for the final meeting. Before that meeting the following factors should be considered:

- Is there compliance?
- The role of intention
- What enforcement strategies are appropriate?

The Judgement of Compliance

Inspecting and auditing to regulations and standards inevitably leads to a judgement on compliance. An assessment of long-term intention and the underlying motivation of those regulated contribute to the compliance decision. However, intention and motivation are not always readily visible or measurable and compliance itself is rarely straightforward. We can help to make sense of these difficult areas by exploring the notion of compliance.

What is Compliance?

Regulations, rules and standards apply to a range of different organisations and situations. For this reason they are broad and probably contain caveats such as 'as far as is reasonably practicable'. If compliance were a simple matter of applying a rule, it could be carried out by a solicitor. However, regulation involves applying a rule in an infinite variety of circumstances. To do this requires the application of expert knowledge, either using knowledge specific to an industry or sector or applying cross-sector knowledge, in the case of environmental regulation, for example. Consequently, regulators usually have a wide degree of discretion, which means having the freedom to choose between courses of action. Discretion in regulation law 'is inevitable because the application of rules, their translation into action, involves interpretation and choice' (Black, 2001: p. 3). Furthermore, the regulator combines this expertise with the authority to enter private domains and obtain information that may be incomplete, not readily available, or withheld.

The evidence gathered to this point is a strong indicator of the degree of compliance. There will still be grey areas that cannot be resolved without liaising with representatives of the organisation and others such as consumers. Nevertheless, a broad idea of where the organisation is compliant and where it is not should now be in place.

Intentions and Future Behaviour

Regulators attempt to build a detailed picture of the 'character' of the organisation, its intentions and likely future behaviour (Black, 2001). Behind these intentions are the motivations of the individuals concerned.

These have been the subject of considerable academic study; the best known of these formulations (Kagan and Scholz, 1984) uses three motivation types:

- **Amoral calculators** use economically motivated models, which are used to determine whether to comply or not based on the costs of compliance or the gains of non-compliance and the risks of detection
- **Political citizens** ordinarily comply with the law but may resist regulations and rules to which they are, in principle, opposed
- **Organisational incompetents** who either do not know the law and rules or else lack the capacity to abide by them.

Perhaps surprisingly, there is agreement that the majority of those regulated wish to comply. As an example, a UK Tax Office survey revealed the following segmentation of individual customers based on:

- Awareness (of one's obligations)
- Motivation (to comply with one's obligations)
- Ability (to comply with those obligations)
- Opportunity (to not comply).

Figure 33: Characteristics of the Compliant and Non-compliant (HMRC, 2009: p. 5)

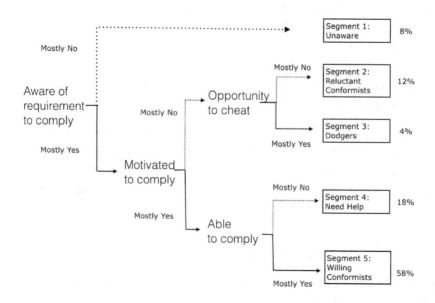

Figure 33 (HMRC, 2009: p. 5) shows that the majority of taxpayers are willing conformists with only a minority who are unwilling. Nevertheless, distinguishing the willing from the unwilling in a relatively short encounter and breaking down willingness to comply into a set of measurable indicators can be difficult. Research (Hutter, 1997, Hawkins, 1984) suggests the following provide a measure:

- The amount of resources devoted by the organisation to achieving the regulatory objectives
- Attitudes of staff towards compliance
- The ability to comply based on skills available and the financial position
- The previous inspection/audit and enforcement records and the nature of any complaints.

Willingness may reflect commitment to the purpose and moral basis of the legislation:

> Regulation in practice, mediated as it is by a bureaucracy in which people have to exercise their discretion in making judgements about their fellows, is founded upon notions of justice ... (inspection) is done in a moral, not a technological world (Hawkins, 1984: p. 207).

Judgement is not only technical, nor is it gathered solely from material evidence. There are complex ethical and moral dimensions. Taking all of this into account suggests that there are three factors at play:

- The **nature** of the non-compliance
- The **willingness** of the regulated organisation to be compliant in the future and
- **Ability** to be compliant in the future.

Figure 34: Compliance Factors

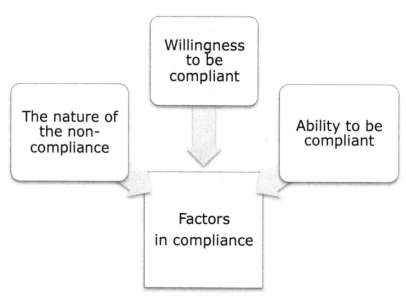

The nature of non-compliance is significant in reaching decisions as to the next step. There may be a need for urgent action, possibly even stopping the inspection/audit if there is the risk of immediate harm. The severity of the risk involved and the probability of it occurring should also be considered.

Figure 35: Willingness and ability

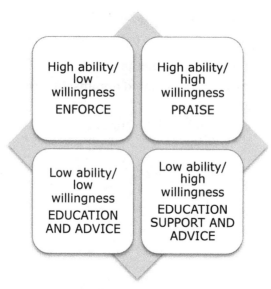

Turning to willingness and ability, Monk (2012: p. 43) (see diagram above)

suggests different choices of inspection intervention dependent on degrees of willingness and/or ability. Those with high ability and high willingness do not need intervention but those with high ability and low willingness do. The bottom two quadrants show low ability to comply and the appropriate strategy here is education and advice.

The Netherlands Ministry of Justice devised a compliance tool known as 'the table of eleven' (Law Enforcement Expertise Centre, 2004) that identifies 'spontaneous compliance dimensions' – characteristics most likely to lead to compliance:

- Knowledge and understanding of the rules
- Financial incentive
- Appreciation that rules are reasonable and fitting to their own situation
- Respect for the authority of the rules (as with the majority who pay taxes)
- Using private/civil/industry-specific standards – the perceived risk of costs resulting from sanction by their own group; for example, the threat of losing quality management system accreditation or failing Good Manufacturing Practice (GMP) standards (USFDA, 2015b).

The above illustrates the features of an organisation that is willingly compliant now and likely to be in the future. Reversing these statements results in characteristics implying that an organisation that will not be compliant in the future.

You are probably wondering why it is that the table contains only 5 points when it is the 'Table of eleven' - the other 6 points refer to enforcement and are worthy of investigation.

Voluntary and Willing Compliance

In reaching decisions on compliance and enforcement, the following strategies can help:

- Become familiar with your legislation – read the original Act. Look for definitions of words and phrases. Sometimes the interpretation offered by additional legislative notes will be useful. Identify the 'spirit' of the legislation. There is an increasing tendency for legislation to commence with a statement of the principles it is based on. These are invaluable in interpreting the regulations, rules and the public interest

- A regulatory or standards body may offer guidance on each of the standards used and the criteria needed to achieve them.

Drawing on Really Responsive Regulation

Further understanding of compliance and strategies for improvement can be achieved by becoming familiar with the principles of 'Really Responsive Regulation' (adapted from Baldwin and Black, 2008). The principles relate to the realities of regulatory decision-making in the changing environment of multiple regulators, self-regulation and civil regulation. Really Responsive Regulation:

- Is flexible towards and tolerant of the use of private standards, self-regulation and to other regulatory bodies
- Aims to analyse the effectiveness of management systems – not just rule violations – to achieve a deeper understanding of how the organisation works and why it performs as it does
- Is alert to new developments and problems e.g. banning of harmful trans-fats in food manufacture (USFDA, 2015a).

From the perspective of Really Responsive Regulation, all regulated sectors are unique and necessitate different compliance strategies and tailor-made improvement tools.

The Psychology of Decision-making

When making compliance decisions, it is worth bearing in mind that not all decision-making is rational. Research suggests that hunches and emotionally-charged situations influence decision-making (Helsloot and Groenendaal, 2011). Two methods of countering these are to:

- Be aware of your own bias and possible reactions to emotional situations
- Enlist the support of a 'devil's advocate', an individual who will challenge beliefs or intentions, perhaps through peer review on a formal or informal basis.

Apply to your work

Think of a compliance decision you made. Did you take into account the nature of the non-compliance, and the willingness and ability of the regulated organisation?

It is inevitable that, as the extent of compliance is evaluated, the appropriate enforcement strategy will also be considered. However, conclusive decisions should not be made at this point, not until the final meeting and feedback session with the organisation. There may have been a misunderstanding or something overlooked during the inspection and the final meeting gives the organisation opportunity to correct or add to the findings – to put their case. It also gives the inspector opportunity to demonstrate fairness.

It is useful to point out that a compliance decision can be made at any point in the process if there is immediate and significant risk to health and safety. Most legislation has within it an allowance for immediate closure or evacuation of an unsafe organisation.

Enforcement

A popular definition of enforcement is 'the use of a legal instrument to gain compliance', but it can also be thought of as a broad process of changing behaviour. Using the latter definition recognises that regulators will sometimes use 'soft' enforcements such as persuasion and warning, and 'hard' enforcement, such as cancellation of a licence.

However, these two approaches have both been found wanting (Gunningham, 2010). The soft approach alone will not deal with the amoral calculators, dodgers or the incompetent who need education and advice. Hard enforcement, when used alone, provokes resistance and negativity, even amongst the majority willing and able to comply, thus creating barriers if pursuing an improvement or risk-based strategy (Gunningham, 2010: p. 125). Rather than seeing soft and hard approaches as mutually exclusive or even as opposing strategies, responsive enforcement brings the two together.

Using this model the regulator will first assume virtue (to which they respond with cooperative measures) but, when expectations are not met, progressively punitive/coercive strategies are justified and can be continued or escalated until the organisation conforms (Gunningham, 2010: p. 121).

Responsive Enforcement

Responsive enforcement (Ayres and Braithwaite, 1992):

- Recognises that both soft and hard approaches are required but, where a hard approach is justified, it must be significant. In the words of Teddy Roosevelt 'speak softly and carry a big stick'.
- Makes the initial assumption that organisations are virtuous until proven otherwise
- Starts with the strategies of advice and persuasion
- Suggests that, where there is non-compliance, the regulator adopts a tit-for-tat approach
- Can be visualized as a pyramid where the regulator selects up and down depending on the response
- The pyramid represents the degree of activity associated with each

type of enforcement – there is more activity at the bottom of the pyramid than at the top (version below by Baldwin et al., 2012: p. 260).

Figure 36:The Responsive Enforcement Pyramid

Nevertheless, while the pyramid (Ayres and Braithwaite, 1992) and the-tit for-tat strategy are influential and attractive to regulators, it has often been difficult to put into practice.

Communication problems between regulators and regulated organisations, as well as institutional impediments, pose difficult challenges to the implementation of the enforcement pyramid. Miscommunication can result from ambiguous, infrequent and interrupted contacts between the regulator and the organisation. It can also result from the lack of organizational or legal infrastructure or because of political or economic pressure rendering it impossible to apply the enforcement style deemed most suitable (Mascini, 2013: p. 53).

Yet, the ideas of responsive enforcement endure, particularly the notion that no one tool fits every job but that the regulator chooses from a range of options (Sparrow, 2000, Sparrow, 2008). This theory marked the end of the sterile debate on soft versus hard approaches, opening the study of regulation to a wider set of theories, notably sociology, psychology and politics.

However, the theory signalled the establishment of a set of skills that did not draw so directly from the public-interest origins of regulation.

Although the responsive regulation of Ayers and Braithwaite has no focus on risk, it opened the way for inspection targeting and risk-based inspection as a means of increasing inspection effectiveness. The driver for this was the conviction that inspection and regulation was a burden on enterprise (Hampton, 2005) even though, as we have seen, the recent expansion of regulation is driven by the demands of the market (Brunsson et al., 2012). Paradoxically, the reduction of the state regulatory burden became synonymous with the public interest.

A separate development of responsive enforcement, 'Smart Regulation' (Gunningham et al., 1998), retained the notion of responsiveness but included in the choice of enforcement are forms of control used by businesses themselves and by third parties, such as standards bodies, the public and pressure groups. The table below illustrates these alternative forms of control (Baldwin et al., 2012: p. 266).

Table 8: Using Alternative Controls

Government as Regulator Controls By:	
Disqualifications	Penal Sanctions
Notices	Warnings
Persuasion	Education
Advice	
Business as self-regulator (private standards) controls by:	
Disqualification	Sanctions
Warnings	Guidance
Education	Advice
Third parties (trade groups, civil bodies) control by:	
Dismissal	Discipline
Promotions	Reviews
Incentives	Training Supervision
Advice	

Many businesses regard reputation as one of their most important assets and safeguard it through ready compliance in order to avoid adverse publicity. Organisations sensitive to risk, safety and reputation will have internal controls that the regulator may trigger. For many firms, compliance with international private and civil standards is essential for their business. Of course, regulatory bodies that can exert influence to *comply* can also exert influence to *improve*. This book began with a definition that encompassed this web of regulation and stressed the importance for all regulators to be aware of the interacting influence of regulation from state, market and civil bodies.

Enforcement Tools

Not all regulators will have the same enforcement tools - some will only have tools specific to a sector. Black and Baldwin identified enforcement tools used by regulators in the US, the UK and Australia. They identified over forty different tools, grouped into seven enforcement action types.

1. Continuation of business/operations – e.g. licence amendments, revocations, disqualifications; imposition of restrictions of activities; seizure of equipment and/or assets
2. Monetary or financial tools e.g. fines, disgorgement of profits orders
3. Restorative tools e.g. remediation orders; restorative conferences
4. Undertaking and compliance management tools e.g. voluntary or enforceable undertakings, compliance assistance; compliance audits
5. Performance disclosure tools e.g. individual naming-and-shaming or league tables
6. Pre-enforcement tools e.g. warning notices to more formal action
7. The role of investigation in prompting compliance (Black and Baldwin, 2007: p. 32).

Dynamics of Enforcement

To understand how enforcement brings about compliance and selects a level of enforcement, there are four models:

- The prospect of enforcement as a spur to drive compliance. The prospect of enforcement action brings compliance, for example the regulator relaying concerns in the final conference
- The financial costs of enforcement to motivate compliance. Compliance is achieved because of the costs involved with an enforcement action (fines, loss of reputation, loss of business)
- The cost of enforcement must be significantly higher than the costs of compliance (new machinery, processing equipment or staff)

- Enforcement bringing public disclosure. The content and impact of enforcement is less important than the shaming and labelling of non-compliance. This is particularly effective where the organisation's image relies on public/corporate responsibility
- Enforcement with one organisation prompts compliance with others. Here enforcement is seen as providing an example to similar firms (Walshe and Phipps, 2013).

Not all regulators have an enforcement function. The Quality Assurance Authority (QAA) in the UK has powers to inspect but has no direct enforcement sanctions. Similarly, standards-based accreditors only have the sanction of cancelling accreditation and removing rights to use standards/logos etc. In the case of international regulation, there are very few cross-border means of enforcement and sanction may occur through consumer action or the withdrawal of recognition (Toffel et al., 2015).

Enforcement Approaches

Figure 37: Seven Approaches to Enforcement

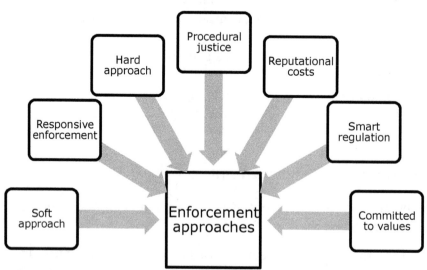

Figure 37 illustrates seven approaches to enforcement. Using a select combination of some, or perhaps all, of these will be most effective. However, we have stressed the importance of the procedural justice approach, not only because it promotes respect and compliance, but also because it offers a demonstrably objective framework for the relationship between regulators and the regulated.

Procedural justice plays an important role in the decision to comply with rules and regulations. Procedural justice:

> Does not rely solely on an instrumental version of cooperation (whereby a person or organization agrees to comply only when they perceive that a positive outcome is likely to result) ... interpersonal relationships and fair treatment by a regulator are more important in nurturing voluntary compliance and deference to rules than relationships that rely on an instrumental tit-for-tat strategy (Murphy et al., 2009: p. 2).

Do I Persuade, Use the 'Big Stick' or Both?

Given the range of enforcements and models the challenge remains to develop enforcement strategies that punish the worst offenders while 'at the same time helping employers to comply voluntarily' (Gunningham, 2010: p. 126). We have seen that the presence of a 'big stick' is a necessary tool for compliance, keeping in line the small minority who refuse to comply and thereby satisfying the feelings of the majority that non-compliers should not be in business on the cheap or 'getting away with it'. However, too much 'hard' enforcement may undermine a general willingness to comply and can be financially costly and disruptive.

> **Apply to your work**
>
> Looking at the section above, what model and/or theory of enforcement does your organisation use? What changes, if any, would you wish to make?

In the majority of cases, compliance is brought about by persuasion and the use of administrative sanctions such as notices and warnings. Enforcement using tools further up the enforcement pyramid is a last resort (Gunningham, 2010).

The Final Conference - Feedback

The purpose of the final conference is:

- To inform the organisation of findings
- To hear and consider the responses to the above
- To continue to extend the principle of fairness and right to reply
- To plan how to address the issues
- To contribute to the organisation's self-evaluation
- To steer improvement strategies – regulatory agencies should 'steer rather than row' (Osborne and Gaebler, 1992).

Many regulators include a formal feedback session or final conference in the inspection schedule (USFDA, 2013: p. 620, Ofsted, 2014). Each regulator differs on the degree of feedback to give and when to give it. Some regulators are cautious, feeling that a premature disclosure of compliance and enforcement decisions may jeopardise the prospect of legal action. Consequently, they advise never to reveal a decision except as provisional. Other regulators expect the inspector/auditor to make final decisions and to include those in the report. There is normally the expectation that any enforcement action is discussed with a regulatory manager before the final report.

The final conference may be cooperative, conflictual or both. Whichever it is, fairness and impartiality should be maintained and procedural justice observed. This means allowing the organisation to hear all the findings and contribute a response before the regulator makes final decisions on compliance and enforcement. Those regulated feel wronged if they see little or no chance to comment or that their comments will be ignored (Nursing Homes Ireland, 2010).

It is constructive to keep to the principle of 'no surprises and no ambush'. If there are compliance concerns, these should have been flagged earlier. It is useful to have a designated contact person to whom information and concerns can be passed during the inspection/audit.

The importance of the final conference should be noted, particularly in relation to risk-management and future compliance. There is an opportunity for working alongside the organisation to improve and go beyond compliance (Gunningham et al., 2004). For those inspected there is value in findings that add to self-evaluation and future performance. Many commentators stress the educational potential of both the inspection and audit (Sanderson, 2001, Rustin, 2004, Smith and Toft, 2005), particularly the role of feedback. For many industries and professions, the reiteration of the principles and values underpinning decisions may promote further improvement (Ehren et al., 2014).

Organising the Conference

It is the regulation team's responsibility to lead and structure the conference's feedback. Who is the feedback to? Where possible, it is advisable to include representatives of those using the regulated services – these may include purchasers and pressure groups, governors and residents of care homes or children's homes. Management members should be present and related roles such as health-and-safety representatives if relevant. However, it should be noted that, if the meeting is too large, frank, clear and open dialogue might be difficult.

From Plan to Feedback to Action Plan

Figure 38: Structuring Feedback

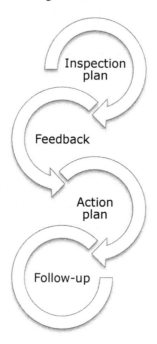

The exact approach will depend on the situation and severity of any non-compliance, but an overview of the inspection/audit plan and a focus on the main issues with brief summaries, would be one approach. It's key to have detailed evidence to hand. If the organisation points to new evidence, it may be possible to incorporate it immediately or it might be necessary to engage in further investigation. Time is a factor but it would be logical to start with the findings of the last report and the success of any action-plan and follow-up before moving on to the present.

Feedback should relate directly to the questions in the inspection/audit plan and not to a specific person. However, where accountability is an issue, it will be preferable to include this at the appropriate time. It is important to be specific about which elements of the standards or controls need improvement but equally important is giving feedback on areas that are functioning well – the results of very few inspections/audits are entirely negative and your feedback should reflect this. Pointing out only the negative is dispiriting and, unless it is fully justified, fails to communicate the whole picture.

It may be necessary to repeat the inspection/audit plan and the evidence-collection criteria and methods so that inspectees are reminded of the criteria you are using. An objective of feedback is to:

- Ensure clarity of the criteria (the standard or principle being used)
- Clarify the difference between the organisation's performance and the criteria
- Work with the inspected organisation to reduce the difference between the performance and the criteria (Schartel, 2012).

> **Apply to your work**
>
> How do you plan for the final conference? Reflecting on previous final conferences you have undertaken, can you list any changes that could improve the experience for you, the end-user and/or the organisation?

Agreeing the Feedback and any Action-plan Requirements

If no agreement on the issues raised is forthcoming, the inspector will need to move on to pre-enforcement and enforcement strategies. Risk, urgency and severity determine the choice of enforcement strategy. Recommendations or simple administrative penalties may be all that is necessary, as with the inclusion of requirements to act contained in a public report. The three important factors to consider are:

- Severity of the non-compliance
- Ability of the regulated organisation to comply
- Willingness of the organisation to comply.

The procedures of many regulators will restrict any final judgement on compliance until there has been further consultation with regulatory agency managers.

> **Apply to your work**
>
> What sanctions and deterrents can you impose on organisations that do not comply? How can you persuade organisations to improve?

Follow-up

The final conference addresses the objectives or outcomes necessary to gain compliance and improvement. All participants should be aware of the likely impacts of the recommendations and/or enforcement action and the preventative action necessary. Follow-up is the means of managing how that is achieved.

Follow-up is an under-researched area of regulation. Weil (1996) cites Siskind (1993) suggesting only 5% of inspections conducted by a large US regulatory organisation were followed-up. The revealing conclusion of Weil's research was that follow-up inspections had a major impact on compliance (1996: p. 635).

Follow-up can be defined as:

> monitoring, analysis/interpretation, management and communication of the outcomes of action planning to remedy non-compliance (Morrison-Saunders et al., 2014: p. 39).

The aims of follow-up include:

- Better project management (controlling)
- Gaining feedback on performance and processes (learning)
- Communicating with stakeholders (informing).

Where outcomes and principles-based standards are used, it is important to verify that the organisation has provided standards and rules that are appropriate and that there are the structures for the monitoring and enforcement of these.

Figure 39: Stages of Follow-up

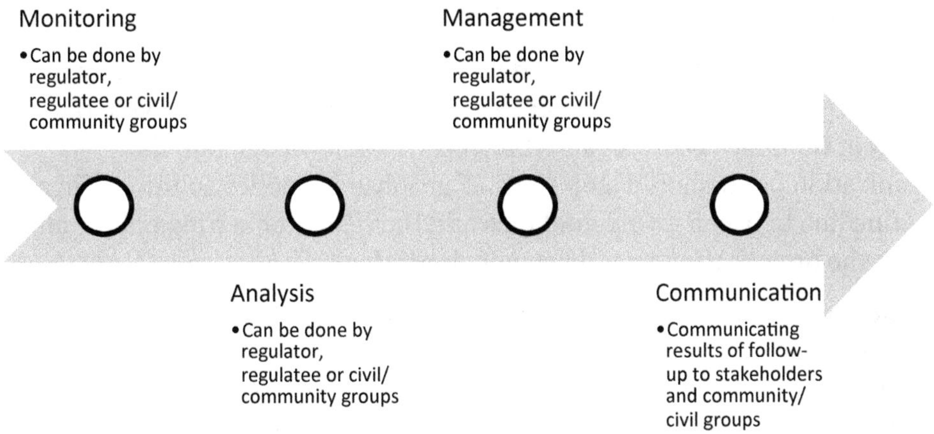

Monitoring
- Can be done by regulator, regulatee or civil/ community groups

Management
- Can be done by regulator, regulatee or civil/ community groups

Analysis
- Can be done by regulator, regulatee or civil/ community groups

Communication
- Communicating results of follow-up to stakeholders and community/ civil groups

Without follow-up the consequences of an action plan are not known until the next audit or inspection. Without follow-up there is no evidence of what went right and wrong and stakeholders remain uninformed.

It is important to specify what is being followed up, who is responsible for completing the work and who is responsible for managing the follow-up. This latter responsibility may be held by one person/organisation or shared between several; independent verifiers may be used (Wessels et al., 2015).

Among the benefits of structured follow-up are:

- Open and transparent communication and cooperation
- Learning and knowledge transfer which improve the competence of regulators, the organisation itself, civil groups and policy makers (Gachechiladze-Bozhesku and Fischer, 2012: p. 26).

The Action Plan

Action Planning is a technique for expressing future actions in terms of either objectives or outcomes so that all parties understand what is required, who will carry out what task and what specific timescales apply. When creating an action plan there are advantages to it being 'SMART':

- **S**pecific (i.e. what specifically is the plan trying to achieve)
- **M**easurable (i.e. the plan must be able to measure the achievement

of the target/goal)
- **A**greed (by all parties involved)
- **R**elevant and Realistic
- **T**ime-bound (realistically achievable timescales).

In most cases, an action plan will detail the actions required to rectify the non-compliance. There may be pressure on the inspector to provide the solution. Guidance is useful and it injects new knowledge into the organisation but it should stop short of proposing a policy solution. There is a fine line between giving guidance and the regulator setting policy, on which the organisation would become dependent.

The action plan should be relevant and realistic. The regulator should be aware of the wider impacts of recommendations, notices and penalties on the organisation. There may be trade-offs to negotiate, such as suggesting employing more staff rather than investing in better financial recording. Similarly, it may be more realistic to stagger certain outcomes rather than set the organisation up to fail. Agreement on the follow-up action plan may be possible at the final conference. Alternatively, it could be agreed that the organisation supplies such a plan later - timescales should be set for this.

The inspection/audit details the performance of the organisation, violations if any and areas of improvement - it contains information that consumers and citizens would find helpful.

Making Information Available

Disclosure

Consumers are at a disadvantage when they do not have all the facts on a product or service. Mandatory disclosure compels businesses and organisations to disclose information that will help consumers make choices. Examples of mandatory disclosure are:

- Statements of true financial position verified by an external body of accountants
- Consumer protection law mandates the publication of accurate, easy to understand information on, for example, interest rates charged by lenders
- Publication of mortality rates (Edwards, 2014)
- Gradings.

Regional and national league tables utilise such disclosed information enabling consumers to compare, contrast and make informed choices. Organisations react to the impact on their reputation either by publication of positive results or, if negative press is warranted, by improvement of a product or service. Failure to improve by the organisation risks continued bad publicity, loss of market share and possible closure.

League tables and regulator oversight provide stronger accountability for performance in industries and services that were previously under local government or state control but are now autonomous.

League tables, used in isolation, will not always reflect the individual strengths of an organisation. For instance, schools have diverse goals, not all of which can be held to account through standardised exam results (Hooge et al., 2012), outcomes such as improved social skills and happy, well-rounded children, for example. Moreover, schools in socially-deprived areas may achieve great improvements in exam-results from a very low base but still come well down an exam-based league table.

Perhaps the best-known form of disclosure is the regulatory report.

Reports

Reports will normally go through a review process before publication. Inspectors should be aware that the consequent possible delay may lead to complaints – some firms rely on up-to-date inspection reports as part of their advertising.

Your organisation will provide a guide to writing the report tailored specifically to your sector.

The Purpose of the Report

- To communicate the methods, conclusions, actions and recommendations to stakeholders including the public
- To provide a starting point for future regulation
- To communicate to managers, customers and end-users the achievement of standards allowing the public a more informed choice
- To demonstrate transparency and accountability making the full report and any summary available online.

Report Quality Criteria

Based on the International Organization of Supreme Audit Institutions (INTOSAI) auditing standards (ECA, 2013b) the quality of the report should demonstrate:

Objectivity

The report should be as unbiased as possible and judged against objective, stated and transparent criteria. It should not mislead and should give regard to both positive and negative aspects without dwelling on or exaggerating either.

Complete

The report should be based on the stated audit/main questions and on any amended or included questions. The reader should be able to see the logical connection between the questions, the criteria, evidence, observations and conclusions.

Clear

The aim of the report should be 'clarity of message'. The report should be easy to read and understand with technical terms and acronyms clarified and explained. The main messages should be easily identifiable and reviewed for ambiguity and misunderstanding. Use of titles and headings makes the report easier to read. Pictures, charts and maps may illustrate complex material.

Convincing

The report should convince the reader of the validity of the findings and conclusions. This is aided by using the inspection and audit main questions and sub questions together with criteria and findings. The conclusions follow logically from these.

Relevant

The content of the report should be relevant to the target stakeholders and should include public interest issues. It should add value to what is already known. It should be timely and not, unless clearly relevant, address dated situations and issues. The report is not a record of all the findings but articulated around the audit questions with the relevant findings and evidence included.

Accurate

Inaccuracy damages the credibility of the report. The evidence should be verifiable and accurately presented.

It is important to distinguish between fact and opinion:

- Facts can be proved
- Opinions are *beliefs* based on one's own subjective views and experiences.

For example,

- OPINION: When I visited WXY Care Home it was grossly understaffed
- FACT: WXY staffing schedule states there should be eight staff on duty between 8am and 8pm. I visited at 10am on 6th July 2014. I saw and could locate only four staff.

Constructive

The report should make practical recommendations for improvement. Where there is weakness, there should be an identification of responsibility to implement improvement.

Concise

The report should be no longer than necessary to support the message and have the maximum impact. Inclusion of too much detail and issues outside the audit/inspection objectives should be avoided.

Targeting the Report

Before the writing of your report commences, it should be remembered for whom it is being written. This will dictate language, tone and vocabulary that will compliment the level of expertise of the reader. The regulating organisation may well guide the inspector as to these elements. The most frequent suggestion is to 'write for the intelligent, non-specialist reader' but this may not be appropriate when writing an inspection report of, for example, a children's home. In a case such as this, two separate reports may be required, one for the management team and one for the children themselves.

Figure 40: Typical Report Outline

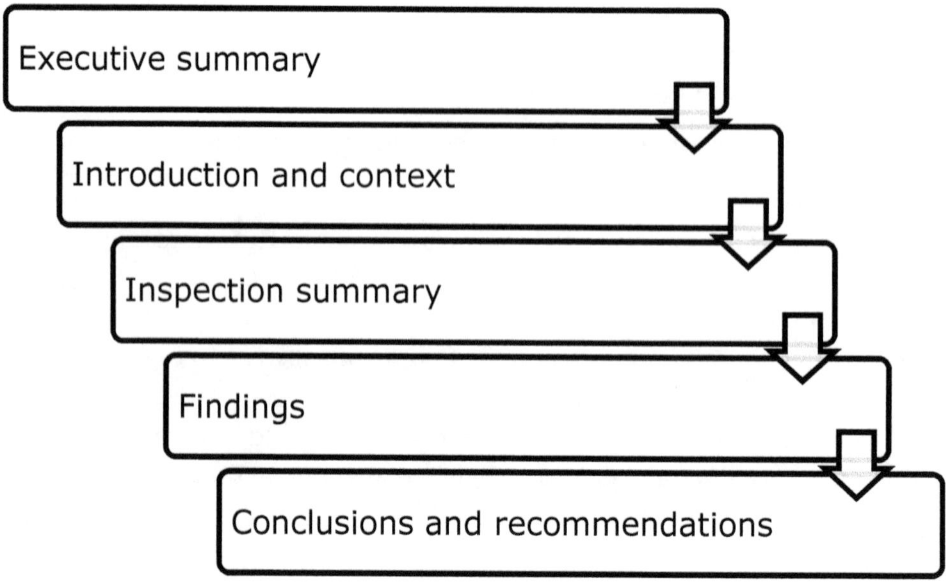

Executive summary

Introduction and context

Inspection summary

Findings

Conclusions and recommendations

Executive Summary

This is for those who do not have the time or the need to read the whole report. It is the most critical part of the report as it is the most read. It should reflect accurately and comprehensively what is in the report. The text should not be too long (around 2 pages) with an emphasis on the main conclusions and recommendations.

It should include:

- Objectives

- Context

- Summarized inspection findings/methods

- Conclusions supported by relevant findings.

The executive summary should stand alone, bringing together the findings from the main body of the report. It should **not** contain information that does not appear in the main body of the report.

Background Information

This may contain:

- Main questions of the inspection/audit
- Principal regulations
- Description of the type of organisation
- Systems and processes of the organisation
- Inspection/audit scope and methodology (detailed information may be included in an annexe).

Inspection/audit Summary

This section describes more fully the process used. It provides specific detail regarding compliance/violation findings and discusses any supporting documentation, clearly explaining issues of concern leading to a recommendation. Any shortfalls link to a *stated inspection method,* supported by evidence.

Findings

It is essential that each area of compliance or apparent violation is clearly set out in this section and not buried elsewhere in the text. The presentation of the findings should help the reader follow the argument.

The following should be apparent to the reader:

- The basis against which the situation was judged, for example, regulations, standards or best practice standards set by the inspector/auditor
- The work done – what was examined
- The findings themselves indicating the source and extent of evidence
- Impact and consequences.

Typically, each standard/requirement and the corresponding findings should be outlined and discussed.

Conclusions and Recommendations

This section provides clear answers to the main questions of the inspection/audit. The conclusions should be more than summaries and should not raise uncertainties or suppositions. They should link to the findings – phrases such as 'it may be' or 'it appears that' are not used.

This section may include gradings or points systems for the organisation – excellent, adequate, poor, if these are used.

This section includes recommendations:

- Regarding changes to correct serious deficiencies
- Addressing the potential for significant improvement (where corrective action is under way it is good practice to point this out).

Recommendations should not be detailed implementation plans, which are the responsibility of management.

The recommendations are likely to achieve greater impact where they are positive in tone and content, are results-oriented (giving some indication of the intended outcome), bear cost considerations in mind and have been discussed and agreed with the auditee (ECA, 2013b: p. 78).

Appendices

Supporting documentation.

Tips for Writing Inspection Reports

- The report should be proofread and checked for clarity by an independent proof-reader

- Use a computer programme for checking both spelling and grammar
- Unless an abbreviation is very common, such as the BBC or UNESCO, full unabbreviated titles should be used at first mention and in abbreviation subsequently
- Use short, direct sentences – they have greater impact
- Use short paragraphs
- Define any complicated terms
- Consult www.plainlanguage.gov for an A-Z of alternative shorter words for unnecessarily long ones
- Avoid language which may cause offence - such as 'children suffering from autism' when 'children with autism' is preferable
- Arial font at 12 with single line spacing is the most popular format.

> **Apply to your work**
>
> You will be familiar with the report format for your own agency. Find examples from different agencies in your own and related sectors. How do they differ from your own and what can you learn from them?

Conclusion

Bad regulation, after all, can do terrible damage to people. Good regulation can control problems that might otherwise lead to bankruptcy and war, and can emancipate the lives of ordinary people. ... Regulation matters ... (Braithwaite et al., 2007: p. 4).

Regulation has changed – the job of the street-level regulator is more complex and demanding than ever. Expectations are often opposing:

- The demand for public safety set against the freedom of regulated firms to innovate and take risks
- Regulators are expected to use professional judgement yet they are required to base decisions on measurable facts
- The citizen is the end-user of regulation yet governments may promote business interests as a priority.

Further, the advent of new types of standards such as performance, outcome and principles-based standards (see Chapter 1) provide advantages but demand greater trust of regulated organisations. As the UK Financial Services Authority chair reflected:

---

principle based standards do not work with those who have no principles (Sants, 2009).

We hope that this book contributes to Braithwaite's notion of good regulation and supports the development of street-level regulatory knowledge. Of course, a book can only contribute if it is read and disseminated: your contribution matters.

References

Aiken, L. H., Sermeus, W., Heede, K. V. D., Sloane, D. M., Busse, R., Mckee, M., Bruyneel, L., Rafferty, A. M., Griffiths, P., Moreno-Casbas, M. T., Tishelman, C., Scott, A., Brzostek, T., Kinnunen, J., Schwendimann, R., Heinen, M., Zikos, D., Sjetne, I. S., Smith, H. L. & Kutney-Lee, A. 2012. Patient Safety, Satisfaction, and Quality of Hospital Care: Cross Sectional Surveys of Nurses and Patients in 12 Countries in Europe and the United States. *BMJ,* 344.

Anderson, S. 2008. *The Anderson Review: The Good Guidance Guide - Taking the Uncertainty Out of Regulation,* London, Better Regulation Executive,

Annakin, L. 2011. *In the Public Interest or out of Desperation? The Experience of Australian Whistleblowers Reporting to Accountability Agencies.* A thesis submitted in fulfilment of the requirements for the degree of Doctor of Philosophy, University of Sydney.

API 2009. *API Recommended Practice 580 Risk Based Inspection.* Englewood: American Petroleum Institute.

Ashby, S., Palermo, T. & Power, M. 2012. *Risk Culture in Financial Organisations: An Interim Report,* London, Centre for Analysis of Risk and Regulation,

Ashworth, R., Boyne, G. A. & Walker, R. M. 2002. Regulatory problems in the public sector: theories and cases. *Policy and Politics,* 30, 195-211.

Aven, T. 2011. On the New Iso Guide on Risk Management Terminology. *Reliability Engineering & System Safety,* 96, 719-726.

Aven, T. 2012. The Risk Concept—Historical and Recent Development Trends. *Reliability Engineering & System Safety,* 99, 33-44.

Aven, T. & Renn, O. 2009. On Risk Defined as an Event Where the Outcome is Uncertain. *Journal of Risk Research,* 12, 1-11.

Aven, T., Renn, O. & Rosa, E. A. 2011. On the Ontological Status of the Concept of Risk. *Safety Science,* 49, 1074-1079.

Ayres, I. & Braithwaite, J. 1992. *Responsive Regulation: Transcending the Deregulation Debate,* New York, Oxford University Press.

Baker, A. 2010. Restraining Regulatory Capture? Anglo-America, Crisis Politics and Trajectories of Change in Global Financial Governance. *International Affairs,* 86, 647-663.

Baldwin, R. & Black, J. 2008. Really Responsive Regulation. *The Modern Law Review,* 71, 59-94.

Baldwin, R., Cave, M. & Lodge, M. 2012. *Understanding Regulation : Theory, Strategy, And Practice, 2nd ed.* , Oxford, Oxford University Press.

Bartley, T. 2011. Transnational Governance as the Layering of Rules: Intersections of Public and Private Standards. *Theoretical Inquiries in Law,* 12, 517-542.

Bartley, T. & Smith, S. N. 2010. Communities of Practice as Cause and Consequence of Transnational Governance: The Evolution of Social and Environmental Certification. *In:* Djelic, M.-L. & Quack, S. (eds.) *Transnational Communities: Shaping Global Economic Governance.* Cambridge: Cambridge University Press.

Baxter, J. & Clarke, J. 2013. Farewell to the Tick Box Inspector? Ofsted and the Changing Regime of School Inspection In England. *Oxford Review of Education,* 39, 702-718.

Bennear, L. S. & Coglianese, C. 2012. *Flexible Environmental Regulation.* Research paper 12-03. Institute for Law and Economics: University of Pennsylvania Law School.

Better Regulation Executive 2009. *Code of Practice on Guidance in Regulation.* London: Department for Business, Innovation and Skills.

Biesta, G. 2007. Why "What Works" Won't Work: Evidence-Based Practice and the Democratic Deficit in Educational Research. *Educational Theory,* 57, 1-22.

Black, J. 2001. Managing Discretion. Penalties: Policy, Principles and Practice in Government Regulation. *ARLC Conference Papers.*

Black, J. 2010. The Rise, Fall and Fate of Principles Based Regulation. LSE Law, Society and Economy Working Papers 17/2010 ed. London School of Economics and Political Science Law Department.

Black, J. 2010b. The Role of Risk in Regulatory Processes. *In:* Baldwin, R., Cave, M. & Lodge, M. (eds.) *The Oxford Handbook of Regulation.* Oxford: Oxford University Press.

Black, J. 2010c. Risk-based regulation: choices, practices and lessons being learnt. *OECD Reviews of Regulatory Reform*, 185-224.

Black, J. 2011. Learning from Failures: *'New Governance' Techniques and the Financial Crisis.* The Regulatory Imagination', presented by the Centre for Socio Legal Studies Regulation Discussion Group in Oxford, May-June 2012. Oxford: Centre for Socio-legal studies Oxford.

Black, J. 2012. Paradoxes and Failures: 'New Governance' Techniques and the Financial Crisis. *The Modern Law Review,* 75, 1037-1063.

Black, J. 2014. Learning From Regulatory Disasters. LSE Law, Society and Economy Working Papers 24/2014: London School of Economics and Political Science, Law Department.

Black, J. & Baldwin, R. 2010. Really Responsive Risk-Based Regulation. *Law & Policy,* 32, 181-213.

Blackburn, S. 2008. *The Oxford Dictionary of Philosophy*. Oxford University Press.

Blanc, F. 2012. *Inspection Reforms: Why, How and with What Results?,* Paris, OECD,

Boyne, B., Day, P. & Walker, R. 2002. The Evaluation of Public Service Inspection: A Theoretical Framework. *Urban Studies,* 39, 1197-1212.

Brady, J. 2010. The Point Is to Change It: Exploring Advice, Guidance and Improvement in the Inspection of Health and Social Care. *European Consortium for Political Research (ECPR), 3rd Biennial Conference: Regulation in an Age of Crisis*. University College Dublin, Dublin, Ireland, 17th-20th June, 2010: ECPR.

Braithwaite, J. 2015. *Responsive Excellence*. Research Paper Prepared for the Penn Program on Regulation's Best-in-Class Regulatory Initiative. Philadelphia: University of Pennsylvania.

Braithwaite, J. & Braithwaite, V. 1995. The Politics of Legalism: Rules Versus Standards in Nursing-Home Regulation. *Social and Legal Studies,* 4, 307.

Braithwaite, J., Coglianese, C. & Levi-Faur, D. 2007. Can Regulation and Governance Make a Difference? *Regulation & Governance,* 1, 1-7.

Brennan, T. A. 1998. The Role of Regulation in Quality Improvement. *Milbank Quarterly,* 76, 709-732.

Brunsson, N., Rasche, A. & Seidl, D. 2012. The Dynamics of Standardization: Three Perspectives on Standards in Organization Studies. *Organization Studies,* 33, 613-632.

Bryman, A. 2004. *Social Research Methods,* Oxford : Oxford University Press,.

Buncefield MIIB 2008. *The Buncefield Incident, 11 December 2005: The Final Report of the Major Incident Investigation Board,* Health and Safety Executive.

Busch, L. 2011. *Standards: Recipes for Reality,* Cambridge, MA, USA, MIT Press.

Busch, L. & Bain, C. 2004. New! Improved? The Transformation of the Global Agrifood System. *Rural Sociology-Baton Rouge-,* 69, 321-346.

Büthe, T. & Mattli, W. 2011. *The New Global Rulers: The Privatization of Regulation in the Global Economy,* Princeton University Press, Princeton.

Carter, S., Mason, C. & Tagg, S. 2009. Perceptions and Experience of Employment Regulation in UK Small Firms. *Environment and Planning C, Government & Policy,* 27, 263.

CDC 2008. *Checklist to Evaluate the Quality of Questions,* Atlanta, Centers for Disease Control and Prevention,

CDC 2008b. *Data Collection Methods for Program Evaluation: Observation.* Atlanta: Centers for Disease Control and Prevention.

CDC 2009. *Data Collection Methods for Program Evaluation: Document Review.* Atlanta: Centers for Disease Control and Prevention.

Clinton, B. 1995. *President's Memorandum on Regulatory Reform: Regulatory Reinvention Initiative.*

Coetzee, P. & Lubbe, D. 2014. Improving the Efficiency and Effectiveness of Risk-Based Internal Audit Engagements. *International Journal of Auditing,* 18, 115-125.

Coglianese, C. 2012. *Measuring Regulatory Performance.* Paris: OECD.

Coglianese, C. 2015. What Volkswagen Reveals about the Limits of Performance-Based Regulation. *REGBLOG* [Online]. Available from: **http://www.regblog.org/2015/10/05/coglianese-volkswagen-performance-based-regulation/** [Accessed 12/10/2015].

Coglianese, C. & Lazer, D. 2003. Management-Based Regulation: Prescribing Private Management to Achieve Public Goals. *Law & Society Review,* 37, 691-730.

COMEST/UNESCO 2005. *The Precautionary Principle.* Paris: World Commission on the Ethics of Scientific Knowledge and Terminology.

Cox, A. L. 2008. What's Wrong with Risk Matrices? *Risk Analysis,* 28, 497-512.

Deloach, J. & Thomson, J. 2014. *Improving Organisational Performance and Governance: How the COSO Frameworks Can Help* [Online]. Durham NC: The Committee of Sponsoring Organisations of the Treadway Commission (COSO). Available: http://www.coso.org/documents/2014-2-10-COSO%20Thought%20Paper.pdf [Accessed June 2015].

Deming, W. E. 1986. *Out of the Crisis : Quality, Productivity and Competitive Position,* Cambridge, Cambridge University Press.

Donabedian, A. 1980. *The Definition of Quality and Approaches to its Assessment,* Ann Arbor, Mich., Health Administration Press, University of Michigan.

Duijm, N. J. 2015. Recommendations on the Use and Design of Risk Matrices. *Safety Science,* 76, 21-31.

ECA 2013. *Guidelines on Audit Interview,* Luxembourg, European Court of Auditors,

ECA 2013b. *Performance Audit Manual.* Luxembourg: European Court of Auditors.

Edwards, M. A. 2014. The Virtue of Mandatory Disclosure. *Notre Dame Journal of Law, Ethics & Public Policy,* 28, 47.

Ehren, M., Perryman, J. & Shackleton, N. 2014. Setting Expectations For Good Education: How Dutch School Inspections Drive Improvement. *School Effectiveness and School Improvement,* 26, 296-327.

EPA 2002. *FIFRA Inspection Manual: FIFRA Interviewing Techniques,* Washington DC, EPA,

EPA. 2015. *DDT – A Brief History and Status* [Online]. US: Environmental Protection Agency. Available: https://www.epa.gov/ingredients-used-pesticide-products/ddt-brief-history-and-status [Accessed 21/03/2016].

Etienne, J. 2013. Ambiguity and Relational Signals in Regulator–Regulatee Relationships. *Regulation & Governance,* 7, 30-47.

Etienne, J. 2014. Different Ways of Blowing the Whistle: Explaining Variations in Decentralized Enforcement in the UK and France. *Regulation & Governance,* Early View Online.

European Committee for Standardization 2005. *Guidance - Standards and Regulations.* CEN.

European Parliament and the Council 2004. Setting Standards of Quality and Safety for the Donation, Procurement, Testing, Processing, Preservation, Storage and Distribution of Human Tissues and Cells. *Directive 2004/23/23/EC.* EU.

European Parliament and the Council 2010. Directive 2010/31/EU The Energy Performance of Buildings. *L 153/27.* Official Journal of the European Union.

Evetts, J. 2013. Professionalism: Value and Ideology. *Current Sociology,* 61, 778-796.

Fairman, R. & Yapp, C. 2005. Enforced Self-Regulation, Prescription, and Conceptions of Compliance within Small Businesses: The Impact of Enforcement. *Law & Policy,* 27, 491-519.

Farrell, M. & Gallagher, R. 2015. The Valuation Implications of Enterprise Risk Management Maturity. *Journal of Risk and Insurance,* 82, 625–657.

Feinstein, J. S. 1989. The Safety Regulation of U.S. Nuclear Power Plants: Violations, Inspections, and Abnormal Occurrences. *Journal of Political Economy,* 97, 115-154.

Feintuck, M. 2005. The Holy Grail or Just Another Empty Vessel? "The Public Interest in Regulation. *Inaugural Lecture.* Middleton Hall, University of Hull: University of Hull.

Financial Conduct Authority. 2015. *Fair Treatment of Customers* [Online]. FCA. Available: **https://www.the-fca.org.uk/fair-treatment-customers** [Accessed 2015].

Fiolleau, K., Hoang, K., Jamal, K. & Sunder, S. 2013. How Do Regulatory Reforms to Enhance Auditor Independence Work in Practice? *Contemporary Accounting Research,* 30, 864-890.

Fisher, R. P. & Geiselman, R. E. 2010. The Cognitive Interview Method of Conducting Police Interviews: Eliciting Extensive Information and Promoting Therapeutic Jurisprudence. *Int J of Law and Psychiatry,* 33, 321-328.

Flynn, M. 2012. *Winterbourne View Hospital: a Serious Case Review.* Gloucester: South Gloucestershire Council.

Francis, R. 2010. *Independent Inquiry into Care Provided by Mid Staffordshire NHS Foundation Trust January 2005 – March 2009 Volume I,* London, House of Commons,

Food Standards Agency. 2016. *Personal Hygiene* [Online]. FSA. Available: **https://www.food.gov.uk/sites/default/files/personal-hygiene-fitness-to-work.pdf** [Acessed 23/03/2016].

FSA 2009. *Scores on the Doors National Website Development Research.* London: COI.

Gachechiladze-Bozhesku, M. & Fischer, T. 2012. Benefits of and barriers to SEA follow-up—Theory and practice. *Environmental Impact Assessment Review,* 34, 22-30.

Gadziala, M. A. 2005. Integrating Audit and Compliance Disciplines within the Risk Management Framework. *Compliance.* New York.

Grace, C. & Fenna, A. 2013. Comparing for Improvement: Recent Developments in Benchmarking. *Public Money & Management,* 33, 235-240.

Graham, J. D. & Noe, P. R. 2015. Beyond Process Excellence: Enhancing Societal Well-Being. *Research Paper Prepared for the Penn Program on Regulation's Best-in-Class Regulatory Initiative.* Philadephia: University of Pennsylvania.

Greenfield, D., Braithwaite, J. & Pawsey, M. 2008. Health Care Accreditation Surveyor Styles Typology. *International Journal of Health Care Quality Assurance,* 21, 435-443.

Gregory, A. H. N. S. L. G. 2011. A Comparison of US Police Interviewers' Notes with their Subsequent Reports. *Journal of Investigative Psychology & Offender Profiling,* 8, 203-215.

Gunningham, N. 2010. Enforcement and Compliance Strategies. *In:* Baldwin, R., Cave, M. & Lodge, M. (eds.) *The Oxford Handbook of Regulation.* First ed. Oxford: Oxford University Press.

Gunningham, N. 2012. Being a Good Inspector: Regulatory Competence and Australia's Mines Inspectorate. *Policy and Practice in Health and Safety,* 10, 25-45.

Gunningham, N., Grabosky, P. & Sinclair, D. 1998. *Smart Regulation : Designing Environmental Policy* Oxford, Oxford University Press.

Gunningham, N., Kagan, R. A. & Thornton, D. 2004. Social License and Environmental Protection: Why Businesses Go Beyond Compliance. *Law & Social Inquiry*, 29, 307-341.

Haimes, Y. Y. 2009. On the Complex Definition of Risk: A Systems-Based Approach. *Risk Analysis*, 29, 1647-1654.

Hampton, P. 2005. *Reducing Administrative Burdens: Effective Inspection and Enforcement*, H.M. Treasury, ISBN: 1 84532 088 3

Hawkins, K. 1984. *Environment and Enforcement : Regulation and the Social Definition of Pollution*, Oxford, Clarendon.

Helsloot, I. & Groenendaal, J. 2011. Naturalistic Decision Making in Forensic Science: Toward a Better Understanding of Decision Making by Forensic Team Leaders. *Journal of Forensic Sciences*, 56, 890-897.

HMRC 2009. *Individuals Prioritisation*. London: HMRC.

Ho, D. E. 2012. Fudging the Nudge: Information Disclosure and Restaurant Grading. *Yale LJ*, 122, 574.

Home Office 2014. *Notebook Guidance*. London: Home Office.

Hood, C. 2006. Gaming in Targetworld: The Targets Approach to Managing British Public Services. *Public Administration Review*, 66, 515-521.

Hood, C. & Peters, G. 2004. The Middle Aging of New Public Management: Into the Age of Paradox? *Journal of Public Administration Research and Theory*, 14, 267(16).

Hooge, E., Burns, T. & Wilkoszewski, H. 2012. *Looking Beyond the Numbers: Stakeholders and Multiple School Accountability*, Paris, OECD Publishing, 1993-9019

Hutter, B. 1997. *Compliance: Regulation and the Environment*, Oxford, Clarendon Press.

Hutter, B. M. & Lloyd-Bostock, S. 2013. Risk, Interest Groups and the Definition of Crisis: The Case of Volcanic Ash. *The British Journal of Sociology*, 64, 383-404.

Interior Health 2008. *Health Protection Mandate Continuum Manual*. Interior Health British Columbia.

International HACCP Alliance. 2015. *International HACCP Alliance* [Online]. Available: **http://www.haccpalliance.org/sub/index.html** [Accessed 10/10/2015].

INTOSAI 2004. *Standards and Guidelines for Performance Auditing Based on Intosai's Auditing Standards and Practical Experience,* Copenhagen, INTOSAI Professional Standards Committee,

ISO Central Secretariat 2008. *ISO 9001 for Small Businesses: What to Do,* Geneva, International Organisation for Standardisation.

ISO 2009. *31000: Risk Management—Principles and Guidelines,* ISO,

James, C. 2011. Whistleblowing, Risk and Regulation. *In:* Lewis, D. & Vandekerckhove, W. (eds.) *Whistleblowing and Democratic Values.* International Whistleblowing Research Network.

Jick, T. D. 1979. Mixing Qualitative and Quantitative Methods: Triangulation in Action. *Administrative Science Quarterly,* 24.

Jin, G. Z. & Lee, J. 2010. The Imperfection of Human Inspectors: Lessons from Florida Restaurant Inspections. Available: **http://www.econ.as.nyu.edu/docs/IO/19018/Jin_03212011.pdf**.

Jin, G. Z. & Lee, J. 2012. A Tale of Repetition: Lessons from Florida Restaurant Inspections. *Working Papers.* University of Maryland.

Jin, G. Z. & Lee, J. 2013. Inspection Technology, Detection and Compliance: Evidence from Florida Restaurant Inspections. *National Bureau of Economic Research Working Paper Series,* No. 18939.

Jin, G. Z. & Leslie, P. 2009. Reputational Incentives for Restaurant Hygiene. *American Economic Journal: Microeconomics,* 1, 237-267.

Johnstone, R., Quinlan, M. & Walters, D. 2005. Statutory Occupational Health and Safety Workplace Arrangements for the Modern Labour Market. *The Journal of Industrial Relations,* 47, 93-116.

Jones, A. & Kelly, D. 2014. Whistle-Blowing and Workplace Culture in Older Peoples' Care: Qualitative Insights from the Healthcare and Social Care Workforce. *Sociology of Health & Illness,* 36, 986-1002.

Jones, K. & Tymms, P. 2014. Ofsted's Role in Promoting School Improvement: The Mechanisms of the School Inspection System in England. *Oxford Review of Education,* 40, 315-330.

Jones, T. F., Pavlin, B. I., Lafleur, B. J., Ingram, L. A. & Schaffner, W. 2004. Restaurant Inspection Scores and Foodborne Disease. *Emerg Infect Dis,* 10, 688-692.

Kagan, R. & Scholz, J. 1984. The Criminology of the Corporation and Regulatory Enforcement Strategies. *In:* Hawkins, J. & Thomas, J. (eds.) *Enforcing Regulation.* Dordrecht: Kluwer-Nijhoff.

Kaml, C., Fogarty, K. J., Wojtala, G., Dardick, W., Bateson, A., Bradsher, J. E. & Weiss, C. C. 2013. The Development of a Standards-Based National Curriculum Framework for Regulatory Food Safety Training in the United States. *Journal of Environmental Health,* 76, 38-42.

Kaptein, M. 2011. From Inaction to External Whistleblowing: The Influence of the Ethical Culture of Organizations on Employee Responses to Observed Wrongdoing. *Journal of Business Ethics,* 98, 513-530.

Kennedy, C. R. 2004. Risk Management in Assisted Reproduction. *Clinical Risk,* 10, 169-175.

Kennedy, I. 2001. *Learning From Bristol: The Report of the Public Inquiry into Children's Heart Surgery at the Bristol Royal Infirmary 1984–1995,* London, HMSO, CM 5207(I)

Kitching, J., Hart, M. & Wilson, N. 2013. Burden or Benefit? Regulation as a Dynamic Influence on Small Business Performance. *International Small Business Journal.*

Klerks, M. C. J. L., Ketelaars, C. a. J. & Robben, P. B. M. 2013. Unannounced, Compared with Announced Inspections: A Systematic Review and Exploratory Study in Nursing Homes. *Health Policy,* 111, 311-319.

Koop, C. & Lodge, M. 2015. What is Regulation? An Interdisciplinary Concept Analysis. *Regulation & Governance,* doi: 10.1111/rego.12094.

Kvale, S. 2006. Dominance Through Interviews and Dialogues. *Qualitative Inquiry,* 12, 480-500.

Lalonde, C. & Boiral, O. 2012. Managing risks through ISO 31000: A critical analysis. *Risk Management,* 14, 272-300.

Lamare, J. R., Lamm, F., Mcdonnell, N. & White, H. 2015. Independent, Dependent, and Employee: Contractors And New Zealand's Pike River Coal Mine Disaster. *Journal of Industrial Relations,* 57, 72-93.

Law Enforcement Expertise Centre 2004. *The 'Table of Eleven': A Versatile Tool.* The Hague: Ministry of Justice NL.

Lord Justice Leveson 2012. *The Leveson Inquiry: An Inquiry into the Culture, Practices and Ethics of the Press,* London, TSO,

Levi-Faur, D. 2011. Regulation and Regulatory Governance. *In:* Levi-Faur, D. (ed.) *Handbook on the Politics of Regulation.* Cheltenham: Edward Elgar.

Lipsky, M. 2010. *Street Level Bureaucracy - Dilemmas of the Individual in Public Services - Updated Edition,* New York, Russell Sage Foundation.

Livingston, A. D., Jackson, G. & Priestly, K. 2001. *Root Causes Analysis: Literature review,* Health and Safety Executive/HMSO,

Makkai, T. & Braithwaite, J. 1992. In and Out of the Revolving Door: Making Sense of Regulatory Capture. *Journal of Public Policy,* 12, 61-78.

Malle, B. F. 2011. Time to Give Up the Dogmas of Attribution: An Alternative Theory of Behavior Explanation. *In:* Zanna, M. & Olson, J. (eds.) *Advances in Experimental Social Psychology, Vol. 44.* Academic Press, Elsevier.

Malloy, T. F. 2010. Social Construction of Regulation: Lessons from the War against Command and Control, The. *Buff. L. Rev.,* 58, 267.

Mandelkern, D. 2001. *Mandelkern Group on Better Regulation Final Report.* Paris: EU.

Martin, S., Downe, J., Grace, C. & Nutley, S. 2013. New Development: All Change? Performance Assessment Regimes in UK Local Government. *Public Money & Management,* 33, 277-280.

Mascini, P. 2013. Why was the Enforcement Pyramid so Influential? And What Price was Paid? *Regulation & Governance,* 7, 48-60.

Mascini, P. & Wijk, E. V. 2009. Responsive regulation at the Dutch Food and Consumer Product Safety Authority: An empirical assessment of assumptions underlying the theory. *Regulation & Governance,* 3, 27-47.

Mattli, W. & Büthe, T. 2003. Setting International Standards: Technological Rationality or Primacy of Power? *World Politics,* 56, 1-42.

May, P. & Wood, R. 2003. At the Regulatory Front Lines: Inspectors' Enforcement Styles and Regulatory Compliance. *Journal of Public Administration Research and Theory,* 13, 117-139.

May, P. J. 2003. Performance-Based Regulation and Regulatory Regimes: The Saga of Leaky Buildings. *Law & Policy,* 25, 381-401.

May, P. J. 2011. Performance-Based Regulation. *In:* Levi-Faur, D. (ed.) *Handbook on the Politics of Regulation.* Cheltenham: Edward Elgar Publishing.

Mcnally, J. S. 2013. *The 2013 COSO Framework and SOX compliance.* COSO.

Mennicken, A. 2010. From Inspection to Auditing: Audit and Markets as Linked Ecologies. *Accounting, Organizations and Society,* 35, 334-359.

Miceli, M. P., Near, J. P. & Dworkin, T. M. 2009. A Word to the Wise: How Managers and Policy-Makers can Encourage Employees to Report Wrongdoing. *Journal of Business Ethics,* 86, 379-396.

Minto, B. 1987. *The Pyramid Principle: Logic in Writing and Thinking,* London, Pitman.

Moeller, R. R. 2013. *Executive's Guide to COSO Internal Controls : Understanding and Implementing the New Framework,* Somerset, NJ, USA, John Wiley & Sons, Incorporated.

Mohammad, M., Mann, R., Grigg, N. & Wagner, J. P. 2011. Business Excellence Model: An Overarching Framework for Managing and Aligning Multiple Organisational Improvement Initiatives. *Total Quality Management & Business Excellence,* 22, 1213-1236.

Monk, J. 2012. *Reform of Regulatory Enforcement and Inspections in OECD Countries,* Paris, OECD,

Moore, K., Kleinman, D. L., Hess, D. & Frickel, S. 2011. Science and Neoliberal Globalization: A Political Sociological Approach. *Theory and Society,* 40, 505-532.

Moran, M. 2010. Regulation and the Financial Crisis. *Biennial Conference of the European Consortium for Political Research Standing Group on Regulatory Governance.* University College Dublin.

Morrison-Saunders, A., Pope, J., Bond, A. & Retief, F. 2014. Towards Sustainability Assessment Follow-Up. *Environmental Impact Assessment Review,* 45, 38-45.

Mortimer, D. & Mortimer, S. 2005. *Quality and Risk Management in the IVF Laboratory,* Cambridge, Cambridge University Press.

Muehlenbachs, L., Staubli, S. & Cohen, M. A. 2013. *The Effect of Inspector Group Size and Familiarity on Enforcement and Deterrence,* Leibniz Information Centre for Economics, 7876

Munro, E. 2004. The Impact of Audit on Social Work Practice. *British Journal of Social Work,* 34, 1075-1095.

Murphy, K., Tyler, T. R. & Curtis, A. 2009. Nurturing Regulatory Compliance: Is Procedural Justice Effective When People Question the Legitimacy of the Law? *Regulation & Governance,* 3, 1-26.

Near, J. P. & Miceli, M. P. 1985. Organizational Dissidence: The Case of Whistle-Blowing. *Journal of Business Ethics,* 4, 1-16.

Nursing Homes Ireland 2010. *High-Level Review of the HIQA Inspection Process for Residential Care Settings for Older People.* Dublin: Nursing Homes Ireland.

OECD 2005. *Guiding Principles for Regulatory Quality and Performance.* Paris: OECD.

OECD 2014. *Regulatory Enforcement and Inspections, OECD Best Practice Principles for Regulatory Policy.* Paris: OECD Publishing.

Office of the Auditor General Canada. 2013. *Sufficient Appropriate Audit Evidence* [Online]. Ontario: OAGC. Available: http://www.oag-bvg.gc.ca/internet/methodology/performance-audit/manual/1051.shtm [Accessed April 2015].

Ofsted 2014. School Inspection Handbook. Manchester: Ofsted.

Osborne, D. & Gaebler, T. 1992. *Reinventing Government,* Reading, MA, Addison-Wesley.

Paoli, G. & Wiles, A. 2015. Key Analytical Capabilities of a Best-in-Class Regulator. *Research Paper Prepared for the Penn Program on Regulation's Best-in-Class Regulatory Initiative.* Philadelphia: University of Pennsylvania.

PETA. 2014. *International Exposé: Sheep Killed, Punched, Stomped on, and Cut for Wool.* Available: **http://investigations.peta.org/australia-us-wool/** [Accessed 24/09/2014].

Powell, M. B., Sharman, S. J. & Cauchi, R. T. 2011. Improving the Quality of Professionals' Contemporaneous Notes Taken During Interviews about Alleged Child Abuse. *Policing,* 5, 317-327.

Power, M. 1994. *The Audit Explosion,* London, Demos.

Price Waterhouse Cooper 2014. *State of the Internal Audit Profession 2014.* PWC.

Public Concern at Work 2013. *The Whistleblowing Commission: Report on the Effectiveness of the Existing Arrangements For Workplace Whistleblowing in the UK,* London, PCaW,

Reason, J. 1990. *Human Error*, Cambridge University Press.

Renn, O. & Graham, P. 2006. *White Paper on Risk Governance: Towards an Integrative Approach*, Geneva, International Risk Governance Council,

Roberts, P., Brown, A. J. & Olsen, J. 2011. *Whistling While They Work: A Good Practice Guide for Managing Internal Reporting of Wrongdoing in Public Sector Organisations*, ANU E Press.

Rosa, E. A. 1998. Metatheoretical foundations for post-normal risk. *Journal of Risk Research,* 1, 15-44.

Rothstein, H. 2003. Neglected risk regulation: the institutional attenuation phenomenon. *Health Risk and Society,* 00005, 85-104.

Rowe, M. 2012. Going Back to the Street: Revisiting Lipsky's Street-level Bureaucracy. *Teaching Public Administration,* 30, 10-18.

Royal Commission on the Pike River Coal Mine Tragedy 2012. *Volume 1.* Wellington, New Zealand.

Rustin, M. 2004. Rethinking Audit and Inspection. *Soundings-London-Lawrence And Wishart,* 86-107.

Ryan, A. M. & Detsky, A. S. 2015. Grade Pending: Lessons for Hospital Quality Reporting from the New York City Restaurant Sanitation Inspection Program. *Journal of Hospital Medicine,* 10, 116-119.

Sanderson, I. 2001. Performance Management, Evaluation and Learning in 'Modern' Local Government. *Public Administration,* 79, 297-313.

Sants, H. 2009. Delivering Intensive Supervision and Credible Deterrence. *Speech by Hector Sants, Chief Executive, FSA The Reuters Newsmakers Event.* London: FSA.

Saunders, M. N. K., Skinner, D., Dietz, G., Gillespie, N. & Lewicki, R. J. 2010. *Organizational Trust: A Cultural Perspective*, Cambridge University Press.

Schartel, S. A. 2012. Giving Feedback – An Integral Part of Education. *Best Practice & Research Clinical Anaesthesiology,* 26, 77-87.

Scott, C. 2010. Standard Setting in Regulatory Regimes. *In:* Baldwin, R., Cave, M. & Lodge, M. (eds.) *The Oxford Handbook of Regulation.* Oxford: Oxford University Press.

Scottish Government 2005. *National Care Standards : Early Education and Childcare up to the Age of 16, Rev. ed,* Edinburgh, Scottish Government.

Simmill-Binning, C., Clough, R. & Paylor, I. 2007. The Use of Lay Assessors. *British Journal of Social Work,* 37, 1353-1370.

Sinclair, D. 1997. Self-Regulation Versus Command and Control? Beyond False Dichotomies. *Law & Policy,* 19, 529-559.

Smith, D. & Toft, B. 2005. Towards an Organization With a Memory: Exploring the Organizational Generation of Adverse Events in Health Care. *Health Services Management Research,* 18, 124-140.

Sparrow, M. K. 2000. *The Regulatory Craft: Controlling Risks, Solving Problems, and Managing Compliance,* Washington, D.C., Brookings Institution Press.

Sparrow, M. K. 2008. *The Character Of Harms: Operational Challenges in Control,* Cambridge, Cambridge University Press.

Swedish National Audit Office 2012. *Performance Audit Handbook.* Stockholm.

Toffel, M. W. & Short, J. L. 2011. Coming Clean and Cleaning Up: Does Voluntary Self-Reporting Indicate Effective Self-Policing? *Journal of Law and Economics,* 54, 609-649.

Toffel, M. W., Short, J. L. & Ouellet, M. 2015. Codes In Context: How States, Markets, and Civil Society Shape Adherence to Global Labor Standards. *Regulation & Governance.*

Toft, B. 2004. *Independent Review of the Circumstances Surrounding Four Adverse Events that Occurred in the Reproductive Medicine Units at the Leeds Teaching Hospitals NHS Trust, West Yorkshire.,* London, Department of Health, 40216

Tombs, S. & Whyte, D. 2013. Transcending the Deregulation Debate? Regulation, Risk and the Enforcement of Health and Safety Law in the UK. *Regulation & Governance,* 7, 61-79.

Tyler, T. R. 2003. Procedural Justice, Legitimacy, and the Effective Rule of Law. *Crime and Justice,* 30, 283-357.

Tyler, T. R. 2006. Psychological perspectives on legitimacy and legitimation. *Annu. Rev. Psychol.,* 57, 375-400.

US Department of Labor. 2003. *Competency Model for Mine Safety Inspector/Specialist* [Online]. US Department of Labor, Mine Safety and Health Administration. [Accessed 2015].

USFDA 2013. *Food Code. In:* Us Department Of Health And Human Services (ed.). Virginia: US Department of Commerce.

USFDA. 2015a. *Final Determination Regarding Partially Hydrogenated Oils (Removing Trans Fat)* [Online]. USFDA. Available: **http://www.fda.gov/Food/ucm292278.htm** [Accessed 21/06/2015].

USFDA. 2015b. *Pharmaceutical Quality/Manufacturing Standards (CGMP)* [Online]. Available: **http://www.fda.gov/Drugs/GuidanceComplianceRegulatoryInformatio n/Guidances/ucm064971.htm** [Accessed 20/06/2015].

Vähäsantanen, K. & Saarinen, J. 2013. The Power Dance in the Research Interview: Manifesting Power and Powerlessness. *Qualitative Research,* 13, 493-510.

Vandekerckhove, W., James, C. & West, F. 2013. *Whistleblowing: The Inside Story—A Study of the Experiences of 1,000 Whistleblowers,* London, UK, Public Concern at Work,

Van Asselt, M. B. A. & Renn, O. 2011. Risk Governance. *Journal of Risk Research,* 14, 431-449.

Vogel, D. 2006. The Private Regulation of Global Corporate Conduct.

Walshe, K., Addicott, R., Boyd, A., Robertson, R. & Ross, S. 2014. *Evaluating the Care Quality Commission's Acute Hospital Regulatory Model: Final Report,* Manchester, University of Manchester Business School, The King's Fund

Walshe, K. & Phipps, D. 2013. *Developing a Strategic Framework to Guide the Care Quality Commission's Programme of Evaluation,* London, CQC,

Weil, D. 1996. If OSHA is so Bad, Why is Compliance so Good? *The RAND Journal of Economics,* 618-640.

Weil, D. 2005. Public Enforcement/Private Monitoring: Evaluating a New Approach to Regulating the Minimum Wage. *Industrial & Labor Relations Review,* 58, 238-257.

Wessels, J. A., Retief, F. & Morrison-Saunders, A. 2015. Appraising the Value of Independent EIA Follow-Up Verifiers. *Environmental Impact Assessment Review,* 50, 178-189.

Wolfe, S., Worth, M., Dreyfus, S. & Brown, A. 2014. *Whistleblower Protection Rules in G20 Countries: The Next Action Plan.* Blueprint for Free Speech, Australia.

Wood, B. D. & Waterman, R. W. 1991. The Dynamics of Political Control of the Bureaucracy. *The American Political Science Review,* 85, 801.

Yapp, C. & Fairman, R. 2006. Factors Affecting Food Safety Compliance Within Small and Medium-Sized Enterprises: Implications for Regulatory and Enforcement Strategies. *Food Control,* 17, 42-51.

Appendix One: Competencies

In **Regulation: Audit, Inspection, Standards and Risk** we identify generic skills and competencies through research literature and regulatory body publications. Regulation knowledge has two elements - see the diagram below. Competency results from the overlap of these.

Figure 41: Regulatory skills and Knowledge

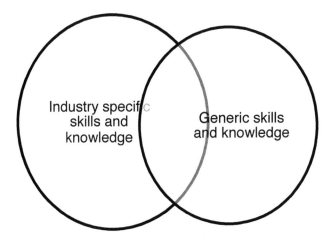

Regulatory Skill Base

There are an increasing number of regulatory competence frameworks. The most significant are listed below with clarification of how the book is relevant:

1. OECD 2014, Regulatory Enforcement and Inspections, OECD Best Practice Principles for Regulatory Policy. Paris: OECD Publishing.

The report recognises core activities including: -

- Evidence-based inspection and audit,
- Use of third parties for compliance,
- Risk focus and proportionality,
- Responsive regulation,
- Fairness of process and
- Increased professionalism of regulators.

The OECD report recommends that:

Inspectors should be trained and managed to ensure professionalism, integrity, consistency and transparency: this requires substantial training focusing not only on technical but also on generic inspection skills, and official guidelines for inspectors to help ensure consistency and fairness (2014: p. 14).

2. Better Regulation Delivery Office, 2014, The Common Approach To Competency For Regulators.

The approach, developed by UK regulators, recognises core and generic regulatory skills. With the exception of IT skills, all are covered in **Regulation: Audit, Inspection, Standards and Risk:**

- Assess risks
- Plan, organise and prioritise
- Promote compliance exercising professional judgement
- Advise and influence
- Conduct interventions
- Enforce relevant legislation

- Work effectively with business
- Work effectively with citizens, partners and stakeholders
- Use and manage knowledge effectively
- Personal development, innovation and learning.

3. International Standards Organisation 2012. 17020:2012 Conformity Assessment -- Requirements for the Operation of Various Types of Bodies Performing Inspection. ISO.

ISO 17020:2012 is a widely used international standard, recently revised, setting out requirements for inspection bodies including their independence and impartiality. The standard makes it clear that inspection:

> normally requires the exercise of professional judgement' ... in particular when assessing conformity with general requirements.

Together with the requirements for ongoing inspector training in methods and techniques the ISO17020 supports the use of required inspection criteria from published standards.

The use of standards, related problems and the processes of evidence-collection and management, are core elements of **Regulation: Audit, Inspection, Standards and Risk:** together with clarity on what is meant by fairness and transparency.

Further relevant curriculum and competency frameworks are given below. For each, this book is relevant.

INECE 2009. *Principles of Environmental Compliance and Enforcement Handbook.* International Network for Environmental Compliance and Enforcement.

Kaml, C., Fogarty, K. J., Wojtala, G., Dardick, W., Bateson, A., Bradsher, J. E. & Weiss, C. C. 2013. The Development of a Standards-Based National Curriculum Framework for Regulatory Food Safety Training in the United States. *Journal of Environmental Health,* 76, 38-42.

US Department of Labor. 2003. *Competency Model for Mine Safety Inspector/Specialist* [Online]. US Department of Labor, Mine Safety and Health Administration. [Accessed 2015].

USFDA 2013. *Food Code,* Virginia, US Department of Commerce, PB2013-110462

CPSIA information can be obtained
at www.ICGtesting.com
Printed in the USA
LVHW021135130722
723396LV00005B/137